Steve,

SEVEN DAYS
IN AUGUSTA

*Thanks for
reading*

Mark Cannizzaro

SEVEN DAYS IN AUGUSTA

Behind the Scenes at the Masters

MARK CANNIZZARO

TRIUMPH
B O O K S

Library of Congress Cataloging-in-Publication Data available upon request

This book is available in quantity at special discounts for your group or organization. For further information, contact:

Triumph Books LLC
814 North Franklin Street
Chicago, Illinois 60610
(312) 337-0747
www.triumphbooks.com

Printed in U.S.A.
ISBN: 978-1-62937-749-0
Design by Nord Compo

To my wife, Carolyn, for her organizational skills
that helped me construct this book and,
more importantly, for putting up with my nonsense.

CONTENTS

Part Four: Thursday

Part Five: Friday

Part Six: Saturday

Part Seven: Sunday

FOREWORD

M y first Masters memory was in 1980 when Seve Ballesteros holed out on 18, chipped in. He was fist pumping. I said to my mom, "I want to win the Masters."

For me, that major championship meant the most because history is made there every year. That was always the most fun tournament to watch, because it was exciting. You had a lot of stuff happening, like birdies and eagles and *fun* golf, the kind of golf I always liked to play.

When I won the Masters for the first time in 2004, it was one of those moments that you kind of realize a dream. When you put stuff out there in the universe and you say, "This is what's going to happen, I'm going to do this," and then you actually do it...that's a cool moment. And that's what was happening for me when I won there for the first time.

You certainly feel differently about yourself as a first-time Masters or first-time major winner, because you know that people are viewing you a little bit differently, or at least you feel it. So you end up having a lot more confidence. It was certainly a validating experience finally winning a major and not having to deal with questions and the criticisms. In a sense it was more of a relief in that regard. But I always knew that it was going to happen, so it wasn't as big a deal.

What I remember most about that day was the Masters used to have a dinner the night of the final round for the winner. You could have all your friends and family and anybody who you want to be there, and that was a really fun experience. I really enjoyed that dinner, because it's your first chance after doing the awards ceremony and giving speeches and doing the media that you can finally relax and hang out with your friends in the Trophy Room. That was always fun.

When I'm asked to compare and contrast my three wins at Augusta, I always say I enjoyed '06 and '10 more, although I remember '04 better because of the moment and the way it all happened.

But I enjoyed the latter two more because I had a two- or three-shot lead walking up 18 and I knew I had it won. I was able to embrace that moment and let my guard down a little bit and look around and take it in. And I still have the memory of seeing the people and walking up the fairway and knowing I had won this tournament. I was able to let myself mentally enjoy it.

That was one of the coolest moments. Don't get me wrong—it's fun to birdie the last hole and win. But you're so in the moment that you don't really have the chance to cherish what's happening. And to enjoy the walk up 18 was pretty special. In '04, I had to stay sharp—and if I don't make par on 18, it's a playoff. I enjoy looking back on '04 more, but I really enjoyed '06 and '10.

The first win, in '04, was probably the most exciting moment in my career—to birdie the last hole to win by one, to win my first major, at the Masters, my favorite event.

The 2010 Masters win for me was special because the entire family was there. My wife, Amy, was past her toughest moments from treatments for breast cancer and the kids were old enough to understand what was going on and enjoy it. When I won my first Masters, my son, Evan, was only one year old. In '10, they were all there. My daughter Sophia and I would go for coffee in the mornings and play chess. The kids were teaching me how to play. I can't believe I hadn't played chess when I was younger, but the kids got me into it. So, we would go to a coffee shop and play chess in the morning, which was a great way to kill some time. I always remember that as being a special part of the week.

After I won in '10 was when I was photographed at a Krispy Kreme drive-thru with the kids while wearing my green jacket. The kids had been asking to go to Krispy Kreme all week long, and I told them, "I'll go, but I can't go until after the tournament. I don't want to have all that sugar in me while I'm playing. But come Monday, I'll unload and eat as much as possible."

So that's what we did. And it worked out very well. I had the jacket on—because I was cold, of course. And the lady there took a picture of it, and there you go. It was all over social media pretty quickly.

My favorite Masters memory before I played the tournament was in 1989, when I was playing college golf for Arizona State and went to Augusta to play a tournament there at Forest Hills. I ended up winning it, which was a cool experience because Bobby Jones had spent a lot of time there. And after that, we went out and watched a Masters practice round at Augusta. I remember seeing Greg Norman and Ray Floyd playing with Jack Nicklaus and Tom Watson. And those four players had the fairways lined on each side down Nos. 8, 9, and 10.

That was the last year that autographs were allowed on the clubhouse side on the golf course, and they all had Sharpie marks all over them. It was chaos. That's what I remember seeing. They could not get from the ninth green to the 10th tee, it was such a mob scene.

The best benefit as a Masters champion is being able to play in the tournament every year until you want to stop. The way they treat the past champions at the Masters is better than any tournament in golf—whether it's the little things like the Champions Locker Room or having the annual Champions Dinner. The way they give you your green jacket to walk around the premises and hang out in, or being able to come back every year, so you get to reminisce on the biggest victory of your career.

You get to be a part of the tournament for the rest of your life. Not every tournament does that.

In recent years, they've started allowing past champions to stay in the cabins at the course. I used to stay in the Marriott Courtyard, and now when I go there, I stay in a cabin. I end up having dinner there, which is brought to the cabin while I watch past Masters Tournaments on the television. They have a system in every cabin where you can call up any of the Masters Tournaments and watch them.

I have watched my wins, but I also like watching the old ones, from Arnold Palmer going back.

It's the memories like that and the chance every year I have to play the Masters that makes it my favorite week in golf. Simply driving down Magnolia Lane still moves me now.

Looking back on it, every time I drive down Magnolia Lane, I drive slower so I can enjoy that moment, because you appreciate it more. When you're young, you think, *Well, I'm going to be doing this all the time.* As you get older, you realize this is a special privilege to be able to drive down Magnolia Lane.

I'm sometimes asked what it will feel like when I play my final Masters as a competitor. It'll be tough. It'll be emotional. But to have had that many years of doing it, and to be a part of the history, is pretty special. So, when it's time, I will have had a lot of great memories and great years.

—Phil Mickelson

PART ONE

MONDAY

Chapter 1

FIRST IMPRESSIONS

You never forget your first look.

The first glance at Augusta National Golf Club is as breathtaking as it is surreal.

The moment you walk through the gates for the Masters Tournament you realize how different it is. For many reasons, it's not like any other golf tournament or sporting event on the planet, but mostly because of the canvas on which the world's most prestigious golf tournament is played.

Augusta National and the Masters are about so much more than the 18 holes, a stately clubhouse, the best players in the world convening once a year, and a trophy being presented to the winner at the end of the week.

It starts with that first look when you've walked through the gates and arrive on the grounds.

Are you in heaven?

Is it real?

Because it seems fake at first glance. It's too perfect to be real.

There isn't a blade of grass out of place. Every piece of grass is emerald green. The pine needles look like they've been carefully combed. The white clubhouse glows at the top of the property and the pristine fairways roll, some like gentle slopes on a ski mountain.

Many have compared it to Disney World for golfers. But Disney World is open to the general public, and it's open all year round. Augusta is available to the general public but for only one week a year and only to those fortunate enough to have scored what is the toughest ticket to attain in all of sports.

Most of the most ardent fans of golf have never stepped foot on Augusta National because they've never been able to get tickets.

Those fortunate enough to get into the Masters marvel at not only the tournament but the vast array of goings on around the city while the tournament is in play.

I'd never dared to dream about getting to Augusta until I took a job at the *New York Post*, became the golf writer and, five months after my first day at my dream job, there I was—covering my first Masters.

Spaniard José María Olazábal won that 1994 Masters, but the end result of that week was so much less significant than the events I experienced that week and the goings on that led up to Olazábal having the green jacket slipped over his shoulders during the awards ceremony on the lawn outside the clubhouse.

There was no such thing as Google Maps or GPS in '94 as I drove down Washington Road looking for the entrance to the club. The sign to enter the property at the beginning of fabled Magnolia Lane is about as large as a cocktail napkin.

Back then, there was a large gravel parking lot in front of the property. It was from that lot you entered through the gates to the golf course. It was there I got my first look, and it was something I'll never forget—the brilliance of the green grass and how perfectly manicured it was.

The experience was not unlike the first time my father took me to a major league baseball game, a Mets–Expos twi-night doubleheader, and I saw the green outfield grass glistening under the stadium lights. It was breathtaking.

The understated buildings, from the clubhouse to the merchandise shop, historical galleries, and the media center—all painted green so they seemed to blend in with the surroundings of the pine trees and nature—blew me away.

The media center was something to behold in its state-of-the-art setup. It looked like a huge college lecture hall, set up like an amphitheater with everything facing a large manual scoreboard and numerous television monitors. Every media member was assigned his or her own seat with audio connections to the TVs and the adjacent interview room.

Those amenities were actually upgraded significantly in 2017, with a new press building built on the back end of the practice facility and looking more like a high-end clubhouse with its own restaurant and locker rooms.

The building features two-story windows that look out at the practice range, a full-service restaurant to go with the walk-up food counter, enormous TVs on the walls, restrooms with attendants, and locker rooms with showers.

Augusta National chairman at the time of the building, Billy Payne, said the club built the facility, which was speculated to have cost some $50 million, out of "the principle of constant improvement. We know no other way."

—

Magic in Those Georgia Pines

This is the rundown of the first four Masters I covered for the *New York Post*.

The first was Olazábal winning after receiving a poignant letter slipped into his locker on the Sunday of the final round from fellow Spaniard and former Masters champion Seve Ball-esteros.

The second was in 1995, when Ben Crenshaw won his second green jacket after having attended the funeral of his swing mentor, the legendary Harvey Penick, in the middle of tournament week. When Crenshaw won on Sunday and collapsed into the arms of his caddie, Carl Jackson, who was a local Augusta National caddie for decades, there wasn't a dry eye on the grounds.

The 1996 Masters was my third, and that was the one in which Greg Norman famously choked away a six-shot lead entering the final round to lose to Nick Faldo in a day that will live in golf infamy, the way the affable Aussie melted down before the eyes of the golf world.

My fourth Masters was '97, when Tiger Woods made history, shattering records and announcing himself to the world as the dominant force he would become for the better part of the next two decades.

After Woods' victory, I began to believe that there was some mystical force that engulfed Augusta National for Masters week. As sports writers, we're trained to root for the best story at the events we cover, because it makes for the best stories to report and write. In the case of the Masters, it seemed (and still does, for the most part, in the 25 Masters I've covered though 2019) that the best story always surfaces.

What is it about the Masters that sets it apart from every other golf tournament, every other sporting event?

"History is made there every year," said Phil Mickelson, who won the 2004, 2006, and 2010 Masters. "It's the only major where that's the case. You might have what some people consider an off year here or there, but so many great memories happen there, because we go back every year. You can't help but walk the place and say, 'Oh yeah, this is the place where so-and-so did this.' Like when Freddie's [Couples] ball stayed up on the bank on '92. It was that moment of destiny, where you kind of knew it was his tournament.

"The biggest thing I remember when I went to Augusta for the first time was being blown away by how hilly it was," Mickelson continued. "Because it doesn't come across that way on television, how straight downhill No. 10 is and how straight uphill 18 is. You don't get a sense for the elevation changes, how difficult the walk up No. 8 is. That hill is long and fairly steep."

Mickelson's favorite Augusta memory—other than the three times he's won the Masters—took place on a week that was not Masters week. It came during a trip to Augusta prior to the 2017 Masters.

"Every year, I go back there and I'll play for a couple of days to get ready before the tournament week. I'll get a group of guys—sometimes it's Tour pros, sometimes it's members of the club, sometimes it's a mixture," Mickelson said. "But before one Masters a couple years ago, I went with Jimmy Dunne and Tom Brady. And we all went and worked out in the morning and Brady said, 'Hey listen, I've got to go throw to [Patriots receiver Julian] Edelman next week. I always like to throw a little bit and keep my arm sharp. Do you mind catching a few passes?'

"So I'm like, 'Hell yeah. Let's do this.' It's 7:20 in the morning and half dark out, he's throwing these passes to me and I've never seen a football come in this hard. I've played catch with some guys with good arms and stuff, but this ball is whistling at me and I'm only catching the last half of it. He's just throwing, just working on it, but he's got such ground force with his feet and his shoulder and the ball just comes in 25 yards away and there's just no drop.

"We were down to the left of the 10th hole in the cottages over there where there's a little gym by the cabins. He's throwing these things in here at me and I've got my fingers bent because I don't want them to hyperextend. I'm making sure the ball doesn't hit my palms, because it'll just bounce off.

"I'm really focused," Mickelson went on. "Those balls were hard to catch. There were three times the ball hit my palm and all three times I had a nerve shot right through my arm all the way throughout my body from these passes. And yet, it's one of my favorite moments, because who gets to catch passes from the freaking greatest quarterback of all time? It had an impact on me, because I didn't realize how hard those balls are coming in and how good those receivers are to catch those things.

"I actually really liked the challenge of it. I just would have liked to do it in daylight when I could see the whole flight of the ball a little bit better."

Paul Azinger, the former player and current broadcaster, recalled not believing what he was seeing when he first walked onto the grounds at Augusta National.

"I was shocked when I saw where the course was in relation to the town and Washington Road," said Azinger, who played in 15 Masters and has broadcast at least as many over the years. "That was the most eye-opening thing to me. When you're coming down Magnolia Lane and you realize how big and old those magnolia trees are it's eye-opening.

"I've always said, 'Nobody who goes to the Masters to play in that event comes in naïve, because we've all seen it on TV all our lives.' And then to have that opportunity to roll down Magnolia Lane as a participant in that event was almost overwhelming. The excitement of it, the butterflies you had, it was awesome."

Azinger said his first look at Augusta National had him feeling like it wasn't real.

"It's like driving into a theme park without all the rides," Azinger said. "It's the most beautiful piece of property in the world and I'll pay $100 to anyone that can find a weed or a clover or anything out of place on the grounds. The agronomy aspect of it is mind boggling. I couldn't wait to get my brothers out there to see it.

"And then you get out there to Washington Road and the traffic jams and you can't even believe the contrast from inside that gate to outside that gate. It's shocking, really. It's an incredible place. Every year I go there it feels like it's not real. It's like everything is manufactured and man-made, but it's not. It's all real. You couldn't create that. God created that and the human hand keeps it pristine."

Azinger's most iconic Masters moment came when he wasn't even at Augusta.

"When Jack [Nicklaus] won in '86, I was actually plying in Hattiesburg, so I missed most of that," Azinger recalled. "In '87, when Larry Mize pitched it in across that green to beat Greg Norman in the playoff, what a moment that was. I remember Freddie's ball staying on the bank [in the 12th hole in the 1992 Masters]. Sandy Lyle getting up and down out of the fairway bunker on 18 [in 1988} was remarkable to me and robbed my good friend Mark Calcavecchia from a chance. I wanted Calc to win so bad.

"And then the Greg Norman collapse there in 1996. It all started in '86 with Greg, some of the heartache at Augusta, losing to Jack. That course was more made for Greg Norman than it was for Jack. I was glad to see Ben Crenshaw win it [in 1995]. That made me really, really happy.

"I was really happy for Trevor Immelman [winning in 2008]. I can remember looking at him thinking he was going to throw up on the fairway somewhere. But he didn't. He hung in there and won it. I was looking at this face, watching him walk. That swing only takes a second or two, the rest of it is, 'Oh my God, can I do this? Can I do this?'

"That's the question you're asking yourself, is, 'Can I do it?' Until you've done it, you don't know. You think you can. Self-belief is critical. You don't know 'til you know."

The lack of a Masters victory on Azinger's resume still eats at him, because he laments the best chance he had in 1998 when he finished fifth and was in the mix right up until Mark O'Meara won.

"I lost by three there, and Mark O'Meara had 11 less putts than me," Azinger recalled. "I played with Mickelson the last day in and I had eight-footer on the last hole. This is what my mind was thinking: 'I cannot believe I'm going to make this and lose the Masters by one.'

"I was heartbroken before I putted it...and then I lipped it out and then O'Meara made that bomb [on 18] and I lost by three. And I was right there. It still crushes me, dude. I think about it all the time. I remember every shot I hit that day. I should have won. Ball striking, I had it. But I couldn't putt into the ocean. For me, it's always the scary memories.

"The golf course can be two things at the same time. It can be a sanctuary and it can be the loneliest place in the world. You cannot call timeout when it's going bad. Not only is there no timeout, you're actually on the clock. It can be the loneliest place in the world."

Despite the 15 times he played the Masters, Azinger said he never mastered the golf course.

"The thing about Augusta is, unlike any place ever, when I played practice rounds, I learned more and more and more about how to play the course," Azinger said. "But at Augusta, the more I learned, the more intimidated it made me. I got worse. I started realizing how dangerous this shot is or that shot is or how in inch this way on No. 15 means the difference in a 12-footer for eagle or hitting back from the other side of that pond.

"The more practice rounds I played at that joint the more it intimidated me and the less of a chance I had to win."

Keegan Bradley's first-impression memory is much more romantic.

"The first time I went I played with my dad," Bradley said. "We flew up there and played with one of the oldest living members. I had never even been on the grounds. It was in March before the [2012 Masters]. It was so stunning. It's very surreal the first time you go there. You walk over that hill on No. 11 and down 10 and there it is. That's it. You can't believe it.

"I was always struck by how close the holes are together. Like you're playing No. 6 and you're walking down looking the 16th green there, or you're playing 17 and No. 15 is right there. It's just so iconic, every second of it. I'd always said I would never play it or go there unless I was playing the tournament. I was able to do that, which was pretty cool.'

For Jim Furyk, like most who are from the Northeast, the Masters is a signal of the arrival of spring.

"Growing up in Pennsylvania, the Masters was the start of the golf season," Furyk said. "That was the event that I was most excited to play for the first time by far. That event has just always been like I imagine it is with how tennis players look at Wimbledon. Everyone tries to copy what Augusta does, the way they run the event. Other events in other places want to be the Masters, because they've set the bar.

"I finished fourth there twice. I was playing with David Duval in '98 and we both missed putts, burned the edge on 18, and Mark O'Meara made his birdie putt there. He beat Duval by one and beat me by two shots. My greatest thrill was standing on the 18th hole at Augusta that year with a putt to tie the lead. That was probably my most exciting moment."

Ernie Els, who's played in 23 Masters, said Augusta National "is a little bit grander now, 25 years later, than it was back then," adding, "But I liked it better then than what it is now. Now they got the whole big practice range, and we don't even go to the old range anymore. We don't even go to the clubhouse that much anymore. When I first went there, the clubhouse was different than what I imagined. It was smaller and simpler, but really cool. The golf course I kind of knew already from watching on television."

Webb Simpson, the 2012 U.S. Open winner, recalled playing Augusta National for the first time when he was 12, playing with his father and his swing coach.

"I'll never forget it," he said. "I shot 80 from the members' tees. Had a blast. It was a lot hillier than I'd imagined and the greens were a lot smaller. On TV, they look pretty big. But they're really small and obviously, I couldn't get over how fast they were."

Jimmy Walker, the 2016 PGA Championship winner, also played with his father the first time he went to Augusta National, in 2009.

"My dad birdied three out of four par-5s," Walker recalled. "We stayed in cabins. I think we stayed in Palmer's cabin. It was amazing. I shot even par on the first day we played, and it was very wet. It played really long. Then the next day, we played in 38-degree weather. I think that's the only place on the planet you will go out and play when it's 38 and drizzling. What a great experience. We played the Par-3 Course. We did it all. It was ridiculous."

Zach Johnson, the 2007 Masters winner, said he first went to Augusta National as a spectator in 2001.

"I was on the mini-tours," Johnson said. "Vaughn Taylor is a good buddy and is from there and he had tickets. I remember walking the golf course, all 18 holes, twice that day. I know I saw Jose [Maria Olazabal] skipping shots off of the pond on 16."

Morgan Hoffmann's first trip to Augusta was to play Augusta State in a college tournament, and while there, he and his teammates got to go to the Masters to see a practice round.

"It was my goal to never set foot on Augusta until I played it for the Masters," recalled Hoffmann, who's played in one Masters, in 2015. But he said his college coach told him, "No, you need to come out and watch the practice round."

"It's a dream come true to be there," Hoffmann said. "It's my favorite course I've ever played. There's nothing like it, the history there. Just walking over some of those bridges. It's really special."

Cameron Tringale, who, like Hoffmann, has played in one Masters (also in 2015), also experienced his first Masters moment as a college player.

"It was my freshman year at Georgia Tech, and I remember driving down Magnolia Lane for the first time and seeing the yellow flowers that make up the logo that's right in front of the clubhouse and thinking, 'Oh my gosh, this is really happening. I'm really going to get to play,'" Tringale said in an interview with PGATour.com. "We cruised slowly. I have no idea what song we played. It could have been gangster rap or opera music. We had a wide range of genres on our team. Someone else was driving.

"I drove later in my career so that I could get the Volvo down Magnolia Lane one time, maybe make it worth more when I sold it. The clubhouse was so different than I thought. It was so classic and so old-school inside. It seemed like it was back in time. I didn't feel uncomfortable, but I definitely was on my best behavior. I remember just wanting to hit the 12th green because everyone was saying how hard it is and I was like, 'No, it's not that hard. It's a 9-iron to the middle of the green.' So I had to hit the green. I hit it on the fringe, just off the green. The first tee shot, too. Talk about nerves for a round that didn't really matter. I wanted to play well so badly."

Brandt Snedeker, too, was moved most by driving on Magnolia Lane to the clubhouse for the first time.

"It was a special experience because of how iconic that lane is," Snedeker said. "I was getting goosebumps, the hair standing up on my arms. Probably the thing that strikes you most is when you walk out of the back of the clubhouse toward the first tee, you see the undulation for the first time and kind of get a view of the whole golf course. You don't realize that on TV. I remember I went for 13 and 15 (in two shots). I knocked it on one of them and hit it in the water on the other. I broke 80, which was the main goal for the day."

Davis Love III recalled playing Augusta for the first time when he was in college at North Carolina.

"We were a bunch of college kids. We were dumbfounded," Love recalled. "I don't think I'd ever played greens that smooth or fairways that perfect. I was scared to hit the ground and take a divot."

Rickie Fowler recalled walking out of the clubhouse and onto the course for the first time and being blown away.

"Seeing it on TV, you don't really understand the routing of the course or what kind of land it's built on, how much movement there is, elevation change," Fowler said. "The thing I remember most is turning in and the guards actually letting me in and driving down Magnolia Lane."

Like Fowler and so many others, Nick Watney said what you see on the TV broadcasts during the tournament do not do the course justice.

"It just seems bigger than it does on TV," Watney said. "The hills are a little more extreme. Everything's a little bit more green and vivid. It's almost like you've got to pinch yourself that you're actually there."

Chapter 2

THE PAPER

The *Augusta Chronicle* might as well be named the *Masters Chronicle*, because there isn't a publication on the planet that has done a better, more thorough and creative job of chronicling the history of the Masters than the local paper.

The *Augusta Chronicle* is the paper of record for the Masters.

Two of the most prolific writers who've chronicled the action are David Westin and Scott Michaux. Westin covered his 41st consecutive Masters in 2019, which also happened to be Tiger Woods' fifth victory, and Michaux was the columnist at the paper from 2001 to 2018.

Westin's forte was writing the daily leads and Michaux the columns. The two of them, along with former sports editor John Boyette, spearheaded the paper's comprehensive Masters Special Section, a project that would begin the Monday after each Masters was complete when Michaux and Westin would convene in the kitchen of Westin's home in Augusta and brainstorm story ideas for the next year.

"David and I would sit down the next morning in his kitchen and we would take notes and write down story ideas of things we were likely to forget before the next Masters year," Michaux said.

"It would be things like Ernie Els had a six-putt on the first hole, or so-and-so played the par-5s in 12-under. Guys who did weird stuff. We would write all that stuff down, because otherwise you forget it. You think you're going to remember it. You think it's all going to be sitting there a year later, but it's not.

"So, we would start divvying things up on famous five-putts at Augusta, little things like that would spark an idea for a story, because when you cover the same tournament every year, if you don't try to make it fresh, it gets boring. That was sort of our little ritual."

That special section was—and still is—the most comprehensive special section for any sporting event you'll ever see. It was so much so that, years ago Westin recalled Hale Irwin grousing about it.

"Hale Irwin once said one of the biggest problems with the Masters is there's just too much pressure because the *Augusta Chronicle* puts out this 80-page Masters edition," Westin recalled. "He was, in effect, saying the paper was overhyping the tournament. That was really kind of a backhanded compliment."

In the early spring leading up to the Masters, Westin and Michaux would show up at the Florida swing events to interview players for profiles they did on every player in the Masters field.

"One year we were at Doral and Nick Price called David Westin the 'Face of Spring,' because when players saw him on the Florida swing, they knew the Masters was right around the corner," Michaux recalled.

Michaux's main project was to write the cover story on the reigning Masters champion, a job that would often take him to the hometown of the player. That meant Australia after Adam Scott won in 2013, South Africa when Charl Schwartzel won in 2011, and Argentina when Ángel Cabrera won in 2009.

"Australia with Scotty was fantastic," Michaux recalled. "He was playing the Australian PGA and it was the first time the green jacket had ever been there to Australia. And the people were obsessed with that thing. You could not imagine an entire country more thrilled. This was one of the great sporting achievements ever in their country. [Ed. note: Scott was the first Australian ever to win the Masters.]

"So, he shows up at the Australian PGA and because we were there, he decided to wear the green jacket out and sign autographs for the kids. People were lined up just go see him and get their picture taken with him and the green jacket. Some people didn't want to touch it, they held it in such reverence."

Michaux recalled Schwartzel as "the most accommodating" of all the Masters champions he profiled.

"He took us up in his plane for a tour around where he lives in South Africa," Michaux recalled. "Then we get into his car and he drives us to the chicken farm where he grew up. He gets us on the tractor, takes us out to tour the entire farm. He walks us through his house, all the pictures on the walls, his bedroom where he grew up, telling all these great stories.

"Now, we've been with him since 7 AM, flown around in his plane, and he says, 'How about we go my house?' It's on the other side of Johannesburg in this posh Gary Player golf community. He had just gotten his helicopter license and he says, 'I'll meet you at my house, and I'll get the helicopter and bring it over.'

"So, he flies the helicopter over the house, lands it in a field. This is the best green jacket picture we ever got. We had Charl Schwartzel in his green jacket with his foot up on the side of the helicopter in the cockpit, headphones on, taking pictures.

"Then he cooks us dinner at his house, just him and his wife and his best friend from school. We had a barbeque, sat around the firepit in his backyard until 10:30 at night. We had now been with him for 16 hours. He was incredible. The most accommodating Masters champion."

The most fascinating—and perhaps harrowing—Masters champion experience Michaux encountered was in Argentina with Cabrera.

"We went to his hometown and visited him at Cordoba Country club, where he caddied and learned the game," Michaux said. "It was important to him to have us for this interview at the place where he grew up as a golfer. He wanted to have an authentic Argentinian asado, which is a barbecue, at a place where he hangs out with all his friends—from the guys that helped him financially when he was getting started as a pro to the guys that worked with him in the caddie yard.

"Unfortunately, it rained a little bit so the cook that was cooking the meat had to do it inside and boiled the meat instead of barbecuing it, and it was delicious. It was like some of the best food I've ever had my life. It was phenomenal. But Cabrera was very upset with him for not having the traditional barbecue that he wanted to have. And he starts sort of like—I think it was playful—chewing out the cook as he's cooking, saying, 'When I asked for an asado, I want an asado.' There was laughter involved, so you weren't quite sure. Cabrera is a very intimidating guy.

"Then at one point, the cook started singing a tango—this sweet, wonderful song about unrequited love and lovers. It was this long, beautiful song, and all these hardened caddies are in the room, crying, listening to it. I mean, it was haunting. It was beautiful, really was amazing.

"Then the food is served. And we're all talking and suddenly, Cabrera says, 'It's time. Let's do this.' And Charlie Epps [Cabrera's coach] tells me, 'Yeah, he wants to do the interview right now.' And I'm like, 'Here? Now? Okay.' So, we're sitting this table and all of these caddies and friends, like 20 of them, are surrounding us at this table, listening in.

"His manager was doing the interpretation for me. It was really intimidating. Cabrera is an intimidating guy to begin with. I know he knows more English than he's willing to participate in. So, the whole thing is in Spanish.

"I felt like I was an FBI agent interviewing Tony Soprano in the back room at Satriale's with Paulie and Silvio and Big Pussy hovering over my shoulder waiting for me to say the wrong thing. It was really, really intense.

"I'm terrified that this is not going to come through on the recorder and this is my one shot with him," Michaux went on. "So it was like 45 minutes of really, the hardest interview I've ever conducted—in the middle of this room with all these guys listening in. And finally, I've just run out of gas and I knew I had some good stuff in there. So, I say, 'Okay, well, I'm done and now we'd like to get a picture of you in the green jacket.'

"Charlie Epps had the jacket there. Our photographer gets up to come over to do this, and Cabrera just goes, 'No.' It was like this sharp, loud, 'No.' It stopped me in my tracks. The way he said, 'No,' we didn't even argue. Cabrera's line was, 'Here, I am Pato. I'm not the green jacket. I'm not the Masters champion. I'm just Pato here.'

"It was a sign of respect to his friends that he was not going to big-time them by putting on the green jacket."

"El Pato," translated from Spanish, means "The Duck," and it's a nickname affectionately given to Cabrera for the way he waddles when he walks.

"So we never got the picture of Cabrera in the green jacket," Michaux said. "He never put it on. We ended up getting a picture of him with a golf shirt on with a PGA of America logo on it. Not even a major championship that he's won. [Ed. note: Cabrera has won a Masters and a U.S. Open]. That was the cover of our section."

Every year on these trips to profile the reigning champion, the one, most important mission demanded by the owner of the *Augusta Chronicle* at the time, Billy Morris (who also happens to be an Augusta National member), was to get a photograph of the player wearing his green jacket.

"Getting the picture of the champion in the green jacket was always Billy Morris' biggest thing," Michaux said. "That's what he wanted the cover shot to be. And it was always a nightmare trying to get these guys to do it. That was one that got away."

Michaux said he was "as emotionally drained and exhausted as I've ever been after doing an interview" when he was finished with Cabrera, and then Epps asked him, "Hey, do you want to go play golf over at Cordoba?"

"I said, 'That would be great, but I don't have any clubs,' and says, 'We'll get you some clubs,'" Michaux recalled. "We were going to play with Charlie's daughter and an old man who was an eight-time Argentine amateur champion. I was like, thank goodness Charlie's daughter is playing. I had gotten to know her over dinner earlier in the week and she's very, very pleasant. What I was unaware of was that she was the runner up in the North-South Amateur Championship once, and I'm like, 'Oh, my God, I am going to embarrass myself in front of these people.'

"We all had caddies and all the caddies had played in the Argentine Open the week before. That's how good they were. The set of clubs they got me was an old set of Cabrera's, an old set of Pings. We get to the first tee and there are all these people watching the guy from 'Au-goosta' play and the caddie hands me this driver and walks away. I look at this driver and it's got a five-degree loft. I'm like, 'Are you kidding me?' So, I naturally, you know, top the heck out of it in front of all these people.

I was like, 'My God, this day couldn't get any more stressful?' I was just out of my league with these guys."

Some of Michaux's subjects were easy, like Scott and Schwartzel. Zach Johnson, after he won in 2007, actually went to Augusta to meet Michaux and did a photoshoot in the famous Magnolia Drive circle in front of the clubhouse.

For all the fascinating experiences, Michaux recalled having some "shit" experiences with his Masters champion cover subjects, too.

"Bubba Watson was weird," he recalled. "We went to Arizona to get him and he was shooting that hovercraft commercial. We go into the clubhouse and I have an hour-and-a-half interview with him, and he was a perfectly good interview. Now we get to the point where we've got to take the picture of him in his green jacket. Bubba swears he had never put it on since the ceremony when he won it. It had been in his closet since. He hadn't taken it anywhere and he hadn't put it on.

"So, we're outside this clubhouse trying to get a picture of him in the green jacket, and he is as nervous as a cat on a hot roof. He is looking around making sure nobody is seeing him in the green jacket. He had that thing on his shoulders for less than 60 seconds. We'd been setting up the lighting and the camera for hours, the photographer had been taking all these practice pictures with me. We had 150 pictures of me so we could get the lighting right.

"And we got about 57 seconds with Bubba in it. He could not get that thing off fast enough. It was as if it was on fire. He didn't want anybody else to see him wearing it. It was one of the strangest things you've ever seen. We had more trouble getting that picture. And that's the picture that Billy Morris wants, that's the only thing he wants."

Michaux said after year after the Masters, Morris would call everyone involved in for a meeting to critique the paper's coverage of that year's tournament.

"Billy Morris brings everyone in and they lay out every page that we put out and he walks around the table and you'd hear, 'I liked this story,' and then, 'I did not like this story,'" Michaux said. "At some point every time, he would say, 'Now, what happened to that green jacket picture?' And I would have to explain why we didn't have it this year. I'd tell him, 'You have no idea how hard it is to get the guy to put on the green jacket.'

"Whenever we didn't get the green jacket shot, we would be flying back from wherever we were and our photographer would just be crestfallen, like, 'I have failed my mission,'" Michaux said. "But I was the only one who always heard about it. I was the one who got yelled at when we didn't have that photo."

In all of the times Michaux chased down Tiger Woods after a Masters win for a profile, they never scored a picture of him in the green jacket.

Michaux also had some curious circumstances with Phil Mickelson after two of the three times he won the Masters.

"We had one year when Phil won it and we shot him at the Tour Championship and he would make sure it was open and you could see the Ford logo on his shirt," Michaux said. "Then we got rules handed to us saying we can't have logos present in the photos with the green jacket.

"Another year Phil won it, I did the interview at Torrey Pines," Michaux said. "He says, 'Meet me in front of the lodge,' and he pulls up in this big old massive Ford SUV and he says, 'Let's do this in my truck.' I'm like, 'Sure, okay.'

"This is right after he was on that subcutaneous fat thing and he was dieting and swore off junk food. He opens the passenger door for me, and the passenger seat is full of McDonald's wrappers and all this McDonald's stuff. He sighed and pulled all the McDonald's stuff out and threw it in the trash.

"I told several people the story and one guy was like, 'That's got to be your lead.' I said, 'Phil's going to win this tournament again. I am not writing about McDonald's wrappers in his truck. I've got to talk to him again.' Every year was an adventure."

Not surprisingly, the most elusive subject was Woods, who almost never grants one-on-one interviews and goes out of his way not to let anyone into his inner circle. So there were no visits to Woods' home or anything intimate like that.

"The first time I did Tiger was in 2001, and I went to Riviera and La Costa [California] to meet him," Michaux said. "You have to just go get him wherever he's playing. In the locker room at Riviera, I talked to Tiger for 10 or 15 minutes. I mentioned I'd be at Match Play the next week.

"Afterward, Tiger saw Mark Soltau, who was his media guy, and he said, 'Tell me about that Scott guy. Who is he? What's his deal?' Soltau tells me this the next day and said, 'I vouched for you with Tiger.' So Tiger was great, perfectly accommodating at Match Play. It was stolen moments. Same thing happened a year later when he won [the Masters] again."

The best interview Michaux ever scored with Woods came accidentally.

"After his win in 2005, I went to Torrey Pines in 2006. I show up there Monday late in afternoon," he recalled. "I stopped by the course to get my bearings and somebody tells me [Augusta native] Charles Howell is out on the back of the driving range. So I run out there to talk to him. Local guy.

"I walk out to back of the range and the only guy there was Tiger. He was with [his coach at the time] Hank Haney. I said, 'This is why I'm here.' I wait 10 minutes and I said, 'Hey, Tiger,' reintroduce myself as I do every time. I said, 'Listen, I'm out here all week. Any time you have to give me here and there would be greatly appreciated. I'm doing the cover story.' He goes, 'How about right now?'

"So, we're standing at his car and Tiger stood there and talked to me for 35 minutes, talking about his father, who passed away later that year, his first Masters, the hate mail he still gets. It was the most personal conversation I ever had with him. Thirty-five minutes into this thing, I said, 'Tiger, I can't thank you enough, but I've got admit, I'm out, I'm tapped out.'

"I couldn't think of anything else to ask him at this point. I said, 'You just made my week and I just got out here.' He said, 'Cool, that's great,' and he walked off. It was a 35-minute one-on-one with Tiger, which was unprecedented back then. It was the best interview I ever had with him."

There always has been a sense of pride on the part of those who put out that *Augusta Chronicle* special Masters section and its daily editions.

"What never got old was that I think people—fellow media members—were impressed by it," Michaux said. "All week long, people were reading that thing in the press room and they were stealing stuff from it. Guys would tell me, 'You're the most plagiarized writer in the world for one week every year.'

"When I took the job there, I thought I was going to be scared shitless trying to write for the *Augusta Chronicle* during Masters week, with everybody in the world there," Michaux went on. "But it turned out, I never was more comfortable doing anything in my entire career. I loved doing that. I knew what I was talking about and writing about. I knew David Westin knew what he was talking about and writing about. And the same for John Boyette.

"We were professionals about it, and I think we put out a good product that people were impressed with. And players would talk about it. Ben Crenshaw would come up to us every year and say, 'I can't believe the work you do. That is the greatest thing in all of newspapers, that section you guys put out every year. And you do it every day for this tournament.'"

For Westin, whose nickname is "Ghost" because his demeanor is so low-key and quiet you sometimes forget he's in the room with you, the *Augusta Chronicle* is all he's known professionally. That led to the 41 consecutive Masters he's covered through 2019.

He spent most of his formative years in Augusta, with his father twice stationed there in the Army. And when Westin got out of college, the paper was the natural fit for him.

"I first went with my dad to the Masters when I was in third or fourth grade," Westin recalled. "He was in the Army and back then, if you showed up in your uniform, you could get into the tournament for free. That's how 'Arnie's Army' started. The servicemen kind of adopted Arnie [Palmer] as their guy, and they would follow him around. So 'Arnie's Army' was a takeoff of that."

Westin recalled the first shot he saw hit was a Tom Weiskopf tee shot into the water on the par-3 16th hole.

The first Masters he covered was in 1979, when Fuzzy Zoeller won the green jacket in his first visit to Augusta. Zoeller remains the last Masters champion ever to win the tournament in his first try.

"Everybody's first Masters, whether as a fan or sports writer covering it, is the one you never forget," Westin said. "That's always the most exciting one. We were in Quonset Hut [the old media center], and all these famous writers were there that I had followed. Herbert Warren Wind was there, just everybody. I was just 23 years old, had gotten out of college in June of '78, so the 1979 Masters [was] my first one.

"I remember I was just so thrilled to be there and whatever story they wanted me to do I will be happy to do it," Westin continued, "I was kind of covering the amateurs and just writing features. We had the afternoon paper at the time. Mr. Morris owned both the *Chronicle* and the *Herald*, but for those first 10 years we had afternoon paper and I would be the guy who'd go there when play started at 7:30 and I had to have a story written by 10:30 in the morning so we had something live from the morning in the *Herald*."

Westin said, through the 41 years, covering the Masters "never got old. Never."

"I don't know how they do it, but it's just like the golf Gods always seem to give us good stories," he said. "I'd say 70 percent of those 41 Masters all had good finishes."

Westin has covered only covered one other major in his career—the 1999 U.S. Open at Pinehurst.

"Back in those days I could have covered them all because we had the budget," he said. "But I was kind of—I don't want to say turned off—but I was disappointed. It was such a letdown to go to another major that wasn't run like the Masters was. My role at the paper was as the Masters expert."

After working as a role player of sorts in the *Chronicle*'s Masters coverage, Westin was asked to start writing the lead stories in 1987.

"My sports editor told me he wanted me to write the lead and I told him didn't want to write the lead, that I like to stay in the background," Westin said. "But he said, 'You're the only one that can do it.' I'm glad I did. It turned out to be memorable because Larry Mize won it, an Augusta native.

"I had been doing sidebars every day on our local guys. So, after the third round, Mize was two shots back of Greg Norman and Seve Ballesteros and nobody gave him a chance. I remember walking to the parking lot with him after his third round. I was only reporter to talk to him. I did a story, and then he wins the tournament the next day [beating Norman in a playoff]. It was my first Masters writing the lead—I've written 114 consecutive daily leads since then—and it was the most exciting."

Westin said his second most vivid Masters memory was in 1986, when Jack Nicklaus won at age 46.

"I saw sports writers running out of the Quonset Hut to go up to the bleachers there on 18 at the time, because they wanted to witness history," Westin said. "They didn't want to see it on TV. It was the only time I've ever seen these old timers like Ed Pope [from the *Miami Herald*] and Art Spander [from the *San Francisco Chronicle*] running to see the winner putt out on 18 so they could say they saw it in person."

A third memory was more of an obscure one.

"I remember Ben Crenshaw was teeing off on No. 1 and I was walking up the hill toward the tee as he was walking down the hill. He looks over and sees me in the crowd and tells his playing partner, 'Hey, there's David Westin from the *Chronicle*, right there,'" Westin recalled. "That made me feel so good. Nobody would ever do that now. He pointed me out like I was some important person."

With the newspaper business in financial peril and continually hurt by the digital revolution, like Michaux after the 2018 Masters, Westin was laid off by the *Chronicle* after the 2019 Masters. He was asked by the paper to freelance for the 2020 Masters. Eventually, though, his Masters run will come to an end, like it does for everybody.

Asked if he can imagine an April in Augusta without being inside the gates of Augusta National covering the Masters, Westin said, "No, I can't. There is a part of you, though, that wonders, 'Wouldn't it be nice to watch it on TV from home and follow it that way?' But you know what? No, it really wouldn't."

Chapter 3

THE LOCALS

C harles Howell III is 19th on the PGA Tour's all-time career money earnings list with nearly $39 million.

And, if not for the Masters, which takes place in Howell's hometown of Augusta, he might never have become a professional golfer.

"I can't imagine that I would have been nearly as interested in the game of golf at a young age had I not lived in Augusta and been around the Masters," Howell said. "There's no doubt the Masters is responsible for me being a professional golfer. There's no doubt about that.

"The Masters, for us as kids, introduced us to the game of golf. And it also made us think of golf as a cool sport to play. A lot of kids are into soccer and football, basketball, but because of the Masters, golf became a cool sport to play. So every year as spring approached, we had a nice reminder and a kick in the tail that to get to working and get to practicing because the Masters was coming back around.

"I remember as kids, our parents would drop us off at Augusta at 9 o'clock in the morning and pick us up at dark. We were just there all day, every day—Monday through Sunday. It was the greatest week of the year. My goodness, I've walked more steps around that golf course. It was just a week that meant so much more than just being a golf tournament. It encouraged us to play the sport."

Howell, whose family were members at Augusta Country Club, which is located adjacent to Augusta National's 12th and 13th holes, recalled the feeling as the circus was about to hit town every year.

"We got excited about it because as it approached and got closer, you'd see the billboards going up around town, you'd see all the things happening and the parking lot signs coming back," he said. "It was more than just a week, because you'd see everything leading into it in the weeks before the tournament's arrival."

Howell's earliest Masters memory is of Larry Mize, also an Augusta native, winning in 1987.

"I was 7 years old at the time, and that was the first year I went to the Masters," he said. "I remember being out there for the playoff [with Greg Norman]. I remember being with my mom and dad off to the right of No. 11 and up on the hill when Mize chipped in and the place just going nuts. I remember that like it was yesterday.

"That probably wasn't good for me, because the first Masters I go to a guy from Augusta wins it. I was like, 'This can happen all the time.' I probably didn't understand at the time and give quite enough credit to how great of an accomplishment that was."

Howell, of course, eventually earned his way onto the PGA Tour and later got to play with Mize.

"Fortunately, we've been paired together a few times early in my career and we've played some rounds together," Howell said. "What a wonderful man he is. He's a great ambassador for Augusta and that golf tournament."

Howell's routine Masters week was pretty simple, and it was a foreshadowing of what he would end up doing for a living.

"I spent a lot of time on the driving range, watching guys, how they practiced, what they worked on, who they had helping them, how they took care of their business," Howell said. "I remembered doing that, because I wanted to be them. I wanted to be out there on that driving range. Sometimes, in practice rounds, I'd pick one guy and follow him all day because I wanted to see how he handled his business."

Eventually, Howell got to handle his own business at Augusta National as a competitor, one of those players he used to watch from the other side of the fence emulating.

In 2002, he qualified for his first of the nine Masters he's played as of 2019, made the cut, and finished tied for 29th. His best finish to date is a tie for 13th in 2004, the year Phil Mickelson captured his first of three career Masters and five career major championships.

"Getting in the tournament, just qualifying for it for the first time, was a bigger deal than even playing in it," Howell recalled. "Qualifying for it for the first time almost felt like winning it. It was such a big deal. Now as I look back on my career, I have a better understanding about just how hard it is just to get the invitation to play in the darn thing. It's just so dang hard to get in the thing, and I definitely appreciate that now. I never took it for granted."

His most memorable Masters moment?

"I remember the first tee shot," he said. "I've never been so nervous in all my life. Never before or since. I just remember the first tee shot. I was so nervous."

Entering 2019, Howell had gone the previous six years without qualifying for the Masters and had played only once (2012) in the previous 10 years. It felt like longer.

Asked if he ever put too much pressure on himself to perform when he was in the Masters field because he is a local, Howell said, "Not really, because the event is such a massive world-wide sporting event. It isn't just a big golf tournament. I've felt the same pressure that everyone else feels because it's the Masters, not because I'm from Augusta."

One thing that six-year drought from 2012 to 2019 taught Howell was never to take it for granted.

"I was 10 the first time I got to play Augusta National," he recalled. "A member of Augusta National was a friend of my dad's. Myself, my dad, the member, and another gentleman from Charlotte played. It was awesome. I still have pictures from it. It was really neat, just to be out there. I played the way forward tees.

"I'd go to the Masters every year and I could see the spectacle of the whole thing. It's a place, for whatever reason, I never took it for granted playing around that golf course. The history of it, you never get tired of it."

Neither did Scott Brown, who also grew up in Augusta and still makes his home in the area, in nearby Aiken, South Carolina.

Like Howell, Brown grew up with the luxury of getting to go to the Masters with his grandfather. And like Howell, those experiences helped turn him into a PGA Tour player.

But unlike Howell, who's played in nine Masters, Brown is still battling to make it into his first Masters field.

"I started going to the Masters as a fan when I was really young," Brown said. "My grandparents had tickets since I was very young. I remember going when I was 5 or 6 years old. I first went to the Par-3 Tournament and that turned into going every Sunday with my granddad until I was 17 or 18 years old."

Brown recalls having aspirations to become a pro golfer and play in the Masters at about the age of eight, saying, "I knew around then that I had a knack for playing good golf and was willing to work hard at it."

He recalled, as a youngster, "For some reason I gravitated to Greg Norman, because he's had so much heartache there. I really wanted him to win one. My earliest memories were watching him, following him and pulling hard for him. The biggest memory I have unfortunately was the six-shot lead he lost in the final round in 1996. My granddad and I would usually sit out on No. 16 every year, and that year we decided we were going to sit on 18 green and watch him finish and win. Unfortunately, we didn't get to see him win."

When he was in high school and early college at University of South Carolina–Aiken, Brown caddied at Augusta National during non-Masters weeks and he said even then there was an aura about the place "that just never goes away."

"Every time you walk onto the grounds out there, it feels ghostly," he said. "It's kind of feels like [deceased club founders] Clifford Roberts or Bobby Jones are going to walk out there from in the trees down by the Par-3. It's like Ted Williams walking out of the dugout. It feels sacred almost."

It, too, is a tantalizing tease for Brown, who's been on the PGA Tour since 2012 and has one career win, but has yet to qualify for a Masters field.

"The biggest goal in my golf life is to play in the Masters, just to play," Brown said. "It's something that I think about quite a bit. I would love to play in the tournament so my granddad can see me play in it one time before he gets older and passes away. It's obviously somewhere that I want to be and play.

"I haven't put pressure on myself to do it, but it is my No. 1 goal. Before my golf career is over, I want to play in at least one Masters. When I'm in contention at other tournaments, I never think about it. I know how hard it is to do, to get into that tournament. It's something that's really hard to do. But I do have enough knowledge of the golf course where I think I can play pretty well in the tournament. From caddying out there and being around it my whole life—watching good shots, bad shots, seeing where they go—I have an intimate knowledge of the golf course."

Brown's home in Aiken is only about a 25-minute drive from Augusta National, yet he never goes there during Masters week, preferring to wait until he's there as a competitor.

"Unless I can get into the field and play the tournament, I'm trying to stay as far away from that gate as possible that week," he said. "I stay at home in Aiken and I'll hang around the house. At Palmetto Golf Club [where he's a member], I have the last tee time in the afternoons, and I'll go out on the golf course at 2 or 3 o'clock and practice and I'll take a cart on the golf course and play and practice during the afternoons.

"Other than playing Augusta National, usually once or twice a year at the most, I haven't been on the grounds during the tournament week since I was 17 or 18 years old."

Brown said he considers himself "lucky" to have witnessed so many historic moments at the Masters as a fan.

"I got to see a lot of cool stuff," he said. "I came along at a good time, where I saw [José María] Olazábal win his first one there, [Ben] Crenshaw did his thing, Tiger did his thing, Phil did his thing. I've seen it all. There's not much more that you can give me that I haven't seen.

"Back when I was a kid, TV coverage wasn't nearly what it is now. I watch it constantly on TV when I'm at home. Now you can follow the leaders from the first hole on. It was special to go with my granddad and he doesn't go anymore. He's older. It's one of those things where it's not as special to go to the tournament like it was when I was a kid.

"Now, I have the opportunity, if I play good and win a tournament, I can actually play in the tournament, which would be really good. I still live here, and it would mean so much more since I am here and still in town to make it into the Masters field."

PART TWO

TUESDAY

Chapter 4

THE DINNER

I t's one of the most exclusive dinner reservations on the planet, and it doesn't even take place on a Friday or Saturday night. It is, however, one night a year.

Tuesday night before every Masters, inside the Augusta National clubhouse, is the annual Champions Dinner. Only past Masters champions are invited. Everyone wears their green jacket. The defending champion is the dinner host every year, and he chooses the menu for the night.

No spouses or media are invited. Honorary invites are extended to the club chairman at the time.

The Champions Dinner was first put into place by Augusta National during the 1952 tournament when defending champion Ben Hogan gave a dinner for the previous winners. Hogan proposed the formation of the Masters Club, with its membership limited to Masters champions.

"I wish to invite you to attend a stag dinner at the Augusta National," Hogan wrote on the first invitation. "My only stipulation is that you wear your green coat."

Stories are told by the players, led by the older generation, and good wine is consumed with the food chosen by the defending champion. If anyone is not satisfied with whatever the defending champion is serving, the regular club menu is available for orders of more traditional dishes like steak, chicken, and pasta.

Patrick Reed, who won the 2018 Masters at age 28, said he had his Champions Dinner menu planned since he was a teenager dreaming of winning the Masters.

"Oh, I knew that back when I was 13," Reed said. "It was always a bone-in ribeye, mac and cheese, creamed corn, creamed spinach. I'm going to fatten those boys up a little bit. I could eat a ribeye steak for breakfast, lunch, and dinner, and mac and cheese, same thing.

"It was a pretty easy decision—it was just kind of refine it a little bit and bring up options where if guys don't want to eat something heavy they have a lighter option as well. I really just want everyone to enjoy the night and have something good to eat, no matter what it is."

The menu choices often reveal something about the player and where he's from.

Scotland's Sandy Lyle, the 1988 winner, famously served haggis in 1989.

"That seemed to make quite a statement," Lyle said at the time. "The older guys, like [Jack] Nicklaus, had been to Scotland and knew what haggis was. But the newer ones, guys like Larry Mize, they weren't too sure about that."

Germany's Bernhard Langer, after his win in 1985, served Wiener Schnitzel in 1986, one of the first international players to serve a dish from his home country.

Canada's Mike Weir, the 2003 winner, served elk in 2004. South Africa's Trevor Immelman, the 2008 winner, served meat pie in 2009. José María Olazábal, after his 1994 win, served paella in 1995. Jordan Spieth, a Texan, served Texas barbecue in 2016 after his 2015 win.

Tiger Woods, after his first win in 1997, served cheeseburgers, chicken sandwiches, French fries, and milkshakes in 1998, when he was just a 22-year-old.

"Hey, it's part of being young," Woods said at the time. "It's what I eat. I was surprised with the number of guys eating the meal. It was a lot of fun—an experience I'll definitely remember for the rest of my life."

Bubba Watson, who won in 2012 and 2014, served the same menu in each of the following years—Caesar salad, grilled chicken breast with sides of green beans, mashed potatoes, corn, macaroni and cheese, and cornbread.

Phil Mickelson's favorite dish in the world is lobster ravioli in a tomato cream sauce, so he served that in 2005 after his first Masters win in 2004.

He raised some eyebrows with his choice of paella in 2011 after his 2010 win, but Mickelson did it to pay tribute to the late Spaniard Seve Ballesteros, a two-time Masters champion who was ill at the time and unable to attend the dinner. So Mickelson's Spanish menu that night included gazpacho, beef tenderloin with Manchego cheese and tortillas, and Spanish apple pie with ice cream.

"All interesting choices that made different statements based largely on personality, geography and the message they were sending to the other champions," Gary Player said. "The South African champions selected a typical braai or barbecue, for example, with some very good South African wines. The international winners love sharing their culture at the dinner, showing how the tournament has grown globally."

Player said he selected his menus to show respect to all players and countries and to take note of how international the Masters has become.

The meals are almost always prepared by the staff of the club kitchen. There was an exception to that after Vijay Singh won in 2000. The club permitted Singh to invite chefs from Atlanta, who imported ingredients from Thailand for chicken Panang curry, sea scallops in garlic sauce, and Chilean sea bass with a chili glaze, served family style. After the meal, Singh brought the chefs to the dining room, where they received a standing ovation.

Mickelson's favorite part of those nights is not what's on the menu, but the conversation.

"Those dinners are usually the chance for the older guys to tell stories," Mickelson said. "Gary Player and Bob Goalby are great storytellers, and they tell some fun stories. It's always fun when Jack [Nicklaus] and [Tom] Watson tell stories, because they always have some good ones of players I watched growing up. Some of us will add some things, but usually it's the older guys telling the stories. I like to listen that week.

"A moment that I remember was Billy Casper, when I won in '06, he told a lot of stories," Mickelson recalled. "That's when I felt really connected to him. He told me a story that was funny: They were playing at Olympic Club in '66 when he won [the U.S. Open]. He was seven shots back playing the front nine and he said Arnold Palmer couldn't have been nicer, saying, 'Come on Billy, let's play a good back side. You can get second place.'

"And Billy ended up shooting 32 on the back to Arnold's 39 and it went to playoff. On No. 18, Arnold had hit his first putt up there and had about a three-footer before Billy had a putt from a similar distance. And Arnold said, 'Do you mind if I tap out?' And Billy said, 'Not at all. Hit it while you're hot.' To me, that's like such awesome, understated smack talk, and I love that. I thought that was one of the best lines."

Mickelson's favorite Champions Dinner story came from Adam Scott's dinner in 2014.

"Adam had this wonderful Australian dinner and out came a Pavlova dessert, kind of an egg white meringue with fruit," Mickelson recalled. "I said, 'Oh, a Pavlova, based off the great Russian ballerina Anna Pavlova. The chef was so inspired by her tutus and beautiful movements he named a dessert for her while she was touring down in Australia.

"Zach Johnson looked at me and said, 'You are so full of it,'" Mickelson went on. "And Chairman [Billy] Payne heard and he said, 'You are so full of it.' I said, 'Well, look I don't know what to tell you. I'll gladly wager $100 on it.' So Chairman looks at me and says, 'You know there's a no cellphone policy here, but it doesn't apply to the chairman.' So, he pulls out his phone and he reads 'Pavlova, inspired after the great Russian ballerina Anna Pavlova while she was touring down in Australia.'"

Mickelson's knowledge on that obscure subject was the result of his daughter, Sophia.

"Sophia was into dance and she had to do a biography on someone, and she did it on Anna Pavlova," Mickelson said with a smile. "And I made 32 Pavlova desserts for her entire class and knew the story. A lot of times I am full of it and get called out on it, but that was one of the times I was not. Every now and then, though....

"Zach Johnson is still in disbelief, which is great."

Mickelson recalled his first crack at hosting the dinner. The night was an equal-parts mixture of pride, laughs, and terror.

"My favorite dish is lobster ravioli in a tomato cream sauce, so that's what I ended up serving, and yet half the guys ended up having a steak," he said. "I didn't even know steak was an option. I realized all the older guys like to have meat. So the other two times I won, I served meat.

"I was nervous about the speech, because I'm speaking to people that I idolized and looked up to—Jack Nicklaus and Tom

Watson and Gary Player and Seve Ballesteros, guys that I watched as a kid growing up," Mickelson said. "Now I'm sitting among them and I'm speaking to them. That was very intimidating."

Byron Nelson used to serve as the dinner's unofficial host for years before Sam Snead took over and then Ben Crenshaw. Mickelson credits Player with being a conversation starter who elicits stories from everyone.

"It is always fun—lots of jokes and stories," Player said. "I used to sit next to Bobby Jones and cut his meat, as his hands were riddled with arthritis. We always joke and laugh about the different menu choices. Some enjoy the different dishes the current champion selects, others choose to order something specific to fit their dietary needs, which is understandable."

———

The Menus

Augusta National does not make the Champions Dinner menus public, but the players almost always tell reporters what the menus are. The following is a sampling of the menus:

Patrick Reed, 2019 dinner: A choice of Caesar salad or wedge salad to start, with the main dish a prime bone-in cowboy ribeye with herb butter (mountain trout was also available for those who prefer fish). Side dish options: macaroni and cheese, creamed corn, creamed spinach, steamed broccoli. Dessert choices: tiramisu, vanilla bean creme brulee, chocolate crunch, and praline cheesecake.

Sergio García, 2018: The menu began with an "international salad," with ingredients chosen to represent the countries of past Masters champions. The entree was arroz caldoso de bogavante, a traditional Spanish lobster rice. And for dessert, García chose his mother's recipe for tres leches cake, served with tres leches ice cream.

Danny Willett, 2017: The Englishman chose a traditional British meal, beginning with mini cottage pies (similar to shepherd's pie but made with beef rather than lamb). The entrée was a traditional "Sunday roast" (prime rib, roasted potatoes and vegetables, Yorkshire pudding). For dessert, apple crumble and vanilla custard. It finished with coffee and tea with English cheese and biscuits, plus a selection of wines.

Jordan Spieth, 2016: Salad of local greens; main course of Texas barbecue (beef brisket, smoked half chicken, pork ribs); sides of BBQ baked beans, bacon and chive potato salad, sautéed green beans, grilled zucchini, roasted yellow squash; dessert of warm chocolate chip cookie, vanilla ice cream.

Bubba Watson, 2013 and 2015: Caesar salad to start. Entree of grilled chicken breast with sides of green beans, mashed potatoes, corn, and macaroni and cheese, served with cornbread. Dessert of confetti cake and vanilla ice cream.

Adam Scott, 2014: An appetizer of artichoke and arugula salad with calamari. A main course of surf-and-turf on the grill, including Moreton Bay "bugs" (lobster) and Australian wagyu beef New York strip steak, served with sautéed spinach and onion cream mashed potatoes. Desserts of strawberry and passionfruit Pavlova, Anzac biscuit, and vanilla sundae.

Charl Schwartzel, 2012: A starter of a chilled seafood bar, which included shrimp, lobster, crabmeat, crab legs, and oysters. The main course was a braai, a South African barbecue that includes lamb chops, steaks, and sausages. Sides of salads, cheeses, sautéed sweet corn, green beans, and Dauphinoise potatoes. Dessert of vanilla ice cream sundae.

Phil Mickelson, 2011: A Spanish-themed menu with seafood paella and Manchego-topped filet mignon as the entrees. Also a salad course, asparagus, and tortillas as sides, plus ice cream-topped apple empanada for dessert.

Ángel Cabrera, 2010: An Argentine asado, which is a multi-course barbecue featuring chorizo, blood sausage, short ribs, beef filets, and mollejas (the thymus gland, also known as sweetbreads).

Trevor Immelman, 2009: Bobotie (a spiced minced meat pie with an egg topping), sosaties (a type of chicken skewer), spinach salad, milk tart, and South African wines.

Zach Johnson, 2008: Iowa beef, Florida shrimp, crab cakes, veal osso bucco ravioli, Iowa corn pudding, and flourless chocolate cake.

Phil Mickelson, 2007: Barbecued ribs, chicken, sausage, and pulled pork with coleslaw.

Tiger Woods, 2006: Stuffed jalapeno and quesadilla appetizers with salsa and guacamole; green salad; steak fajitas, chicken fajitas, Mexican rice, refried beans; apple pie and ice cream for dessert.

Phil Mickelson, 2005: Lobster ravioli in tomato cream sauce, Caesar salad, garlic bread.

Mike Weir, 2004: Elk, wild boar, Arctic char, and Canadian beer.

Tiger Woods, 2003: Porterhouse steak, chicken, and sushi and sashimi; salads, crab cakes, asparagus, mashed potatoes, and a chocolate truffle cake.

Tiger Woods, 2002: Porterhouse steak and chicken with a sushi appetizer.

Vijay Singh, 2001: Seafood tom kah, chicken Panang curry, baked sea scallops with garlic sauce, rack of lamb with yellow kari sauce, baked filet Chilean sea bass with three-flavor chili sauce, lychee sorbet.

Mark O'Meara, 1999: Chicken fajitas, steak fajitas, sushi, tuna sashimi.

Tiger Woods, 1998: Cheeseburgers, chicken sandwiches, French fries, milkshakes.

Nick Faldo, 1997: Fish and chips, tomato soup.

Ben Crenshaw, 1996: Texas barbecue.

José María Olazábal, 1995: Paella, hake, and tapas.

Bernhard Langer, 1994: Turkey and dressing and Black Forest torte.

Fred Couples, 1993: Chicken cacciatore with spaghetti.

Sandy Lyle, 1989: Haggis (a Scottish specialty of minced sheep organs—heart, liver, and lungs—with minced suet, oatmeal, and onions, then boiled inside a sheep's stomach) with mashed potatoes and mashed turnips.

Bernhard Langer, 1986: Wiener Schnitzel and Black Forest cake.

Chapter 5

THE TOWN

John Daly has called Augusta "the greatest town in America this week," referring, of course, to Masters week.

"Then," he wryly added, "everybody tells me it's a little dead after that."

Such is the reputation of Augusta, which happens to be the second-largest city in Georgia after Atlanta, about a two-and-a-half-hour ride away.

During the seven days in Augusta that represent Masters week every April, the town becomes a bustling metropolis overrun by golf fans, tourists, and opportunists trying to make a quick buck.

"Augusta is really your typical southern town," Scott Michaux, a former columnist for the *Augusta Chronicle*, said. "It's the second-largest city in the state of Georgia and it's got plenty of industry, it's got poverty, it's got wealth. It is a very normal southern city. It's not Savannah and Charleston with a tourist industry. It doesn't have any of that...except one week of the year. Golf is its one defining element. And the rest of the year it's just a normal southern town."

Michaux, who lives in Athens, Georgia, but helped spearhead the Masters coverage for the *Chronicle* for years, resents the bad reputation Augusta gets when it's not Masters week.

"Everybody makes the comments about Washington Road," he said of the infamous main drag on which Augusta National resides. "There's literally a Washington Road in every city. Every significant city in America has its own Washington Road, a road with car dealerships, chain restaurants, strip malls, strip joints.

"People make fun of Augusta because of Washington Road. I say to people, 'Your town has a Washington Road. But you know what your town doesn't have? It doesn't have Augusta National on your Washington Road or your Main Street or your Broad Street or whatever you call it. You don't have that club on it.'"

Washington Road has become a lightning rod for ridicule because of the stark contrast of culture when it comes to the world's most famous and exclusive golf club, playground to the privileged, sitting in the midst of the cheesy chain restaurants, auto dealerships, gas stations, and strip malls.

"I don't think people in Augusta are embarrassed by Washington Road," Michaux said. "They're proud that they have a world-class, internationally-recognized event as their franchise. The Masters is their franchise. The Masters defines that city. I live in Athens, where the University of Georgia drives that city. The Masters, even though it's one week a year, is the most important engine that Augusta has. People call it the 'Second Christmas.' It's the 53rd economic week of the year. It's the economic boom of the year.

"Augusta National doesn't always like that people are profiting off their event, but people make money renting their house, people are making money catering. There's so much money to be made Masters week that it is the single most important thing of the year.

"People base their kids' college education on the money they collect from renting their homes that week. This is how they pay their mortgages. It's really a massive economic generator for the whole town, and people are proud of it.

"Some of those people have never been to the tournament. They live in Augusta their whole lives and they've never been inside those gates. But they identify with that tournament, because in one way or another they're benefiting from it."

For the first Masters I covered for the *New York Post*, in 1994, I stayed at a Days Inn on Washington Road, about two miles away from Augusta National, and paid $225 per night. When I checked out after my seven days in Augusta, I asked the front desk clerk how much it would cost me for the night if I needed to stay there the Monday after the tournament. I was told $25.

This was my earliest experience of the price gouging that takes place during Masters week.

Brian Bush is a real estate closing attorney who grew up in Augusta, has his business there, and still lives there. He's been a part of the Masters house-renting culture since he was a kid, when his father rented the family house for the week.

"I was raised in Augusta for all my life that I can remember, and everyone has always rented houses out for Masters week, including my family when I was young," Bush said. "I remember we would pack up the house before Masters week and get out of Dodge. Sometimes, we would even help the people coming in to rent with coordinating things. I remember going to the liquor store with my dad and buying box after box after box of alcohol for the people coming in, because they'd sent him money and a shopping list. It was crazy.

"We had a house that was walking distance from the course and my dad was able to rent his house for quite a handsome

sum of money every year, so we used that money to go on family vacations."

Asked if the rental income for the week can cover a year's
mortgage, Bush said, "Probably not a year, but you could definitely make a substantial dent in the mortgage, yeah."

Bush pointed out that a lot of the hotels and motels along
Washington Road serve as residences for many people.

"They have people that literally don't have a home so they
use the hotels as their residence and they pay by the week," he
said. "And, when it comes time for Masters week, they get a
little notice slipped under the door that says, 'You are going to
vacate the premises before Masters week or you are going to pay
what the Masters people are paying, which is 10 times what you
are paying.'

"So, all those people are homeless for the week unless they
can find a friend to shack up with, because they can't afford the
amount that the Masters renters are paying for that week. The
hotels are charging prices that are phenomenally higher than what
they charge for the rest of the year."

Bush said the city becomes "frenzied" in the weeks leading
up to the Masters week "because so many people are doing what
we do, which is getting our house ready for guests coming in."

"You're doing massive spring cleaning; it's spring cleaning
on steroids," he said. "Then the businesses are doing the same
thing—they're gearing up for a major change. The restaurants
are throwing away every menu in the house and printing up new
ones because they want to raise the prices for Masters people
coming in. The hotels are going crazy.

"Anybody that's in any kind of service industry at all is getting
geared up or they're getting the hell out of Dodge and making
room for someone who might just want to rent their parking lot

for the week. It's just a massive change of the entire vibe of the city leading up to Masters week."

After Masters week?

"It's like nothing ever changed; it's instantaneously back to normal," Bush said. "I do not understand how it changes so quickly, but it does. Everybody is just whipped and tired and it does get pretty mellow."

Scott Brown, an Augusta native who's a member of the PGA Tour, recalled watching the buildup to Masters week as a kid anticipating it.

"I see everything that leads up to it when I'm at home," Brown said. "You can start to feel it in the air around February and definitely by the first of March people start talking about it. It's different when you're around it.

"When it's not Masters week, it's just a normal town," Brown went on. "There's not much here sports-wise. There's a Single A baseball team here [the Green Jackets]. There's no sporting events going on except for that one week a year other than the baseball team. That's all we've got. At all these other cities where we have tournaments, there's basketball and baseball and football. They have that all year long. We've got one thing, one time a year. And it just happens to be the biggest golf tournament in the world."

Bush said he clears out of his downtown office for Masters week every year.

"I'm never here Masters week, it's always blocked off on the calendar," he said. "As far as any kind of real business happening for me Masters week, it's pretty much nonexistent. Nobody expects to have a house closing on Masters week. It would be like having closing on Christmas Day. It's not going to happen."

There are a lot of normal goings on that cease in Augusta during Masters week. Among them are funerals. Even funerals are put off during Masters week.

The *Newark Star-Ledger* did a story quoting the owner of Platt's Funeral Home in Augusta saying business is "deader than usual" during Masters week. It's not that people don't die during tournament week, it's just that their burials are delayed until after the final putt disappears underground.

"Everything revolves around the tournament in this town, and that includes funerals," Herb Gilstrap from Platt's told the paper.

———

The Lone Home

Herman and Elizabeth Thacker are longtime Augusta natives who have steadfastly refused to allow Augusta National and its little annual golf tournament to disrupt their lives. So much so that the Thackers have refused to sell their property, at 1112 Stanley Drive, to Augusta National as every one of their nearby neighbors did in the mass purchase the club started making in 1999 to create almost 300 acres of empty fields to use for parking the one week the tournament occupies on the calendar.

With every other family in the neighborhood having sold their homes to the club for an inflated price, the Thackers are the lone holdouts. And the house they've lived in since they built it in 1959, which now happens to be adjacent to Augusta National's Gate 6-A, remains a beacon amongst the vast emptiness 51 weeks a year.

According to the *Wall Street Journal*, Augusta National spent some $200 million to buy more than 100 homes on about 270 acres of land adjacent to the club, which has more than doubled the size of the club's footprint.

The Thackers' house is listed at about 1,900 square feet, has three bedrooms, and sits on about two-thirds of an acre. According to the real estate database, it has an estimated value of

$261,000, yet Augusta National has made offers to the Thackers of well over $1 million to buy their home and bulldoze it.

"We really don't want to go," Elizabeth Thacker told the *Newark Star-Ledger*.

"Money ain't everything," Herman Thacker told the paper.

The Thackers raised their two children, five grandchildren, and five great-grandchildren in that house.

In an interesting twist, the Thackers' grandson is Scott Brown, the PGA Tour player and an Augusta native. He still spends time with them at the house as he did when he was a kid and went to the Masters with his granddad.

"I go see them quite often, all the time," Brown said. "I'm pretty close to my grandparents, they pretty much raised me. I would stay with them as much as I could. Growing up over there was really special, right in the heart of it during Masters week."

Brown now is amused by the bizarre look when it's not Masters week and his grandparents' home sits by itself in the middle of all those acres of unused land.

"It looks like a 300-acre farm," he said. "Other than about two weeks prior and during the tournament it's pretty much like their own personal playground. For 50 weeks of the year, it's like their own farm."

While Herman Thacker's brother sold his two houses to the club for a reported $3.6 million, Brown said he fully understands why they refused to relent as every one of their neighbors did in the big sellout.

"They've been there more than 60 years," Brown said. "They used to own two houses—one across the street. I lived there when I was in college, and they sold that one [for a reported $1.2 million]. I had a feeling after they sold that one, they wouldn't sell their home. They were 75 or 76 years old at the time. I know their personality. I know they love that area. They had done well for themselves in their career.

"I didn't think the first money that was offered was going to sway them into moving. Obviously, those numbers have gone up and they ended up selling the one across the street. I don't remember what the highest offer was, but it was definitely in the millions after the first offer was about $300,000. By them holding out, it was a good move. They were lucky. They didn't need the money where they were like, 'We're not going anywhere now.'"

Herman Thacker said he still gets an occasional visit from an Augusta National member.

"He'll come by here every so often, and he'll say, 'Just want to let you know we're still interested in your property,'" Thacker said. "And we'll tell him the same thing again."

Brown said his grandparents "looked" for another home in case they opted to sell "but could never find anything in that area they fell in love with."

"They're definitely not going to sell now," he said. "They're 85, 86 years old now. They're not going anywhere now. Whoever the house is willed to will have to make that decision when the time comes and they've passed on."

Brown, who has never played in a Masters because he has yet to qualify, praised how Augusta National members and officials have treated his grandparents.

"Augusta has done a great job with making them feel comfortable in that atmosphere," Brown said. "They've come and planted magnolias around the property, where they are still kind of secluded in the parking lot where nobody can come onto their property. They've done a really good job of making them feel comfortable even though they didn't sell the house to them. They could have been the total opposite. They could have made it like, 'We're going to do everything we can to make these people sell by making them feel uncomfortable.' But they've done the exact opposite."

There is no end to Augusta National's land grab. The club continues to purchase land and expand.

"People had homes there for decade after decade after decade and now those homes are no longer there," Brian Bush, the Augusta real estate attorney, said. "But those were $60,000 or $70,000 homes and Augusta National paid those people $300,000 and $400,000 for them and those people were able to sell those little rinky-dink, run-down pieces of crap and go buy a really nice house in a good neighborhood."

Bush remains amused by the Thackers' holdout.

"It's hilarious," he said. "The guy is still out there holding out and doesn't have any interest in selling. He's going to stay there until he's dead."

Chapter 6

THE TREE

The oldest living member of Augusta National has never struck a golf ball, donned a green jacket, eaten a pimento cheese sandwich, or sipped on a Masters Punch on the clubhouse veranda.

The oldest living member of Augusta National, however, has seen and heard more than anyone who's ever attended the Masters Tournament.

The oldest living member of Augusta National is the massive oak tree that sits between the iconic white clubhouse and the first tee. The tree, which is believed to be more than 160 years old, serves as an unofficial monument not only to Augusta National, but to the game of golf.

During Masters week, everything takes place underneath that oak tree. Everyone who is anyone in golf passes through the welcoming shade the gigantic branches provide on those hot April Augusta days. And they don't merely pass through: they linger, they chat, they schmooze, they booze, they ogle.

Players pass through on the way to their rounds and again after their rounds en route to the locker room. Journalists interview players under the tree. Player agents strike deals under the tree.

The only thing that does not take place under that gigantic tree, whose trunk is as thick as a VW bus, is golf. You'd have to hit a pretty errant drive off the first tee for the big oak tree to come into play.

"When you think of landmarks around the world—the Statue of Liberty, Mount Rushmore—this is the Mount Rushmore and Statue of Liberty of golf," former player and current broadcaster Peter Jacobson said. "This tree could tell you stories all the way back to Bobby Jones, Ben Hogan, Sam Snead, and Byron Nelson. This has been the scene of unbelievable joy and incredible sadness and heartbreak, right under this tree.

"If this tree could talk..."

If the tree could talk, it might be able to offer some insight as to why Clifford Roberts, the Augusta National chairman from 1931 to 1976, decided to walk down to Ike's Pond on club property and take his life at age 83 with a gunshot in 1977.

The tree sits directly in the path between the clubhouse and the first tee and practice putting green. So it serves as a constant path for players either going to play or returning to the clubhouse after playing.

At any moment, Jack Nicklaus might amble by with his wife, Barbara. So too might Phil Mickelson, Condoleezza Rice, Nancy Lopez, Rory McIlroy, or Jordan Spieth.

At the 2005 Masters, during the height of Tiger Woods' dominance, minutes before his Sunday afternoon final-pairing tee time, he marched past his mother, Tida, who was standing under the tree to encourage her son before he went out to battle. Woods never broke stride and never looked at Tida, instead staring straight ahead in a trance. He was focused on the task at hand, which was winning his fourth green jacket.

Which he did.

"As far as networking, there is no better place in golf," 2006 U.S. Open winner Geoff Ogilvy said. "Anybody who is moving or shaking anything in golf is standing here this week."

Nathan Grube, the longtime tournament director for Travelers Championship in Hartford, Connecticut, makes the pilgrimage to Augusta every year for the Masters. Not to see the tournament, but to build and manage valuable relationships under the oak tree.

"An hour at the tree is worth a week at the office," Grube said. "The entire ecosystem of golf is there—players, managers, PGA Tour officials, media officials. It's a pretty special place, that tree."

Current and former U.S. presidents have congregated under that tree. So too have star professional athletes across leagues.

In a moment of conversation under the tree during the 2019 Masters, NFL Commissioner Roger Goodell, who's an Augusta member, told two reporters a funny story about one of his Masters experiences. Goodell, speaking about how thorough and diligent the club is about manicuring the pristine grounds, recalled a morning when he was awakened at 4:00 AM by an army of workers blowing leaves and pine needles outside of the cabin he was staying in on the club grounds.

He said he couldn't go back to sleep so he walked outside of his cabin in his boxer shorts, took a seat on a bench at one of the tee boxes, and quietly took in the beauty of the club in the pre-dawn serenity before the place would begin to bustle with patrons gathering around the golf course and the movers and shakers in the game under the oak tree.

"The business deals that are to be done here, people that we've met when designing golf courses around the world, we meet here," three-time Masters winner Gary Player said. "Any business deals, international, right here. International friends, you meet here."

Jay Danzi, Jordan Spieth's manager, called the tree "a unique place," saying, "Everybody in the golf world meets under the tree. It's where everyone goes. It's one of the most special places in golf. I hope it's there forever."

"Before I came here the first time, I had heard all about this landmark tree," 1998 Masters winner Mark O'Meara said. "If you say, 'Under the oak tree,' people know what you're talking about."

NBC Sports and Golf Channel announcer Jimmy Roberts called the tree "the initial destination for everybody I know."

"I told somebody who has never been here: 'I'll meet you at the Tree,'" Roberts recalled. "He said: 'The tree? That's like telling somebody in Manhattan, 'I'll meet you at the car.' I said: 'You will know what I'm talking about when you get there.'"

Lives have changed under that tree. Ask Fuzzy Zoeller, the 1979 Masters winner and the only player in the tournament's history to win a green jacket in his first try.

It was under that tree Zoeller conducted that fateful TV interview during Tiger Woods' record-setting 1997 Masters victory, when he was excoriated for being racially insensitive.

A 21-year-old Woods was en route to winning his first Masters, shooting a record 18 under par to become the first African American to win a major professional golf tournament. Zoeller, always known as one of the most affable, free-speaking jokesters in the sport, stood under the tree speaking to reporters after finishing his final round of the tournament.

Among the group of reporters was a camera crew for CNN.

With a drink in hand, Zoeller famously said of Woods, "That little boy is driving well and he's putting well. He's doing everything it takes to win. So, you know what you guys do when he gets in here? You pat him on the back and say congratulations and enjoy it and tell him not to serve fried chicken next year. Got it?"

Then, after a smile, Zoeller added, "or collard greens or what-ever the hell they serve."

Zoeller was referring to the annual Masters Champions Din-ner, in which the previous year's winner gets to select the menu.

The fallout from Zoeller's remarks was swift and harsh. His largest sponsor, Kmart, immediately dropped him without even a conversation with him. He quickly became the poster child for racism in sports, which was unfair.

Woods, declining to take some dozen calls from Zoeller in the immediate aftermath, iced him, leaving him to twist in the wind for three days before he finally released a statement through his man-agement company that coolly acknowledged Zoeller as a "jokester" who likely didn't mean anything malevolent by the remarks.

Zoeller's life, since that fateful moment under the old oak tree, was never the same.

"It's been tough," Zoeller said at the time. "Tough for my family. Tough for me. It hurt me. It cut me right in half. I thought my first back surgery was painful, but nothing like this. It seemed that all I had worked for in 22 years was suddenly gone.

"I've been out there 22 years and, if for some reason I'd been on the other side of the ledger, I'd have picked up the phone in five minutes and called the guy," Zoeller went on. "That's just because of my respect for the Tour and the players. There are lot of other guys out there who would have done the same thing. Even the commissioner [Tim Finchem] was trying to reach Tiger about this.

"I've been on the tour for 23 years and anybody who knows me knows that I am a jokester. It's too bad that something I said in jest was turned into something it's not. But I didn't mean anything by it and I'm sorry if I offended anybody. If Tiger is offended by it, I apologize to him, too. I have nothing but the utmost respect for Tiger as a person and an athlete."

Said fellow player Tom Lehman: "I know Fuzzy, and it was obvious to me that he was attempting to be funny. He probably would have said the same thing to Tiger's face and they both would have yukked it up... [but] it wasn't the best timing, and it wasn't in good taste. It's not appropriate."

The years have softened the sharp blows Zoeller's life took from the fallout of his comments in 1997.

On the eve of the 2017 Masters, Zoeller was back under the oak tree again, holding an empty Masters cup with a green swizzle stick in it and joking with reporters.

"I was just standing here with a drink in my hand and Arnold threw some shit down at me from up in the tree," Zoeller said with a smile in reference to Arnold Palmer, who'd died a year earlier yet whose presence was still felt. "I looked up and said, 'Arnold, is that you?' Because I was drinking a vodka, but it wasn't Arnold's brand, Ketel One."

PART THREE

WEDNESDAY

Chapter 7

PAR-3 CONTEST

"Magic happens down there."

Those are words Ernie Els used to describe the Par-3 Course at Augusta National, where on the Wednesday of every Masters week they conduct the annual Par-3 Contest, which is more popular to many people than the golf tournament itself. The Wednesday ticket for Masters week has become perhaps more coveted and expensive in the ticket aftermarket than the one for the final round on Sunday.

The course is located to the right side of the clubhouse and is carved into a valley with two ponds and elevated tees. On Wednesday the course is lined with patrons, 10 deep in some places, as people crane their necks to get a glimpse of the world's best players and some legends in a completely casual, fun setting with no green jacket on the line.

Players often have their kids or spouse caddie for them, all dressed up in the traditional white overalls.

"I think the members might go fishing there or have a drink out there and then, come Wednesday, there's 30,000 people down there," Els said. "It's quite something. It's really cool. The whole thing is unbelievably cool. It's set up to make a lot of holes-in-one."

Indeed, the holes are intentionally cut in places on the greens where balls feed to, in hollows and valleys, and there are usually at least a few holes-in-one each year.

"In 2017, with Jack Nicklaus almost winning the thing and then Gary Player was almost winning the thing, and then Jack's grandson gets a hole-in-one," Els recalled. "That can only happen there. It's just a place of magic."

The thing that's not magic about the Par-3 Contest is this: since the event was added to the Masters week itinerary, no player who's ever won the Par-3 Contest has gone on to win a green jacket that week.

That's a fact, or superstition, that's not lost on players. Some skip the contest altogether because of it. Some purposely hit shots into the water late in the contest if they are in or close to the lead. Some intentionally disqualify themselves from turning in an "official" card by letting their kids, partner, or even someone they've pulled from the gallery putt for them.

Only Ben Crenshaw and Vijay Singh have won a Par-3 Contest and eventually gone on to win the Masters, but never in the same year. The closest any player has come to breaking the hex was in 1990, when Raymond Floyd won the Par-3 but lost the Masters in a sudden-death playoff, won by Nick Faldo.

Jimmy Walker owns the Par-3 Course record from his 8-under-par finish in 2016.

The most magical days of the Par-3 took place before Arnold Palmer died. Palmer, Nicklaus, and Gary Player—the Big Three—traditionally played the Par-3 together and drew massive crowds. Nicklaus and Player still pair up together and have added Tom Watson to their threesome.

In 2018, Nicklaus' 15-year-old grandson, GT, jarred a shot on the ninth hole and brought the grandfather of 22 grandchildren to tears.

Nicklaus tweeted afterward: "With all due respect to the Masters, allow me to put my 6 green jackets in the closet for a moment and say that I don't know if I have had a more special day on a golf course....To have your grandson make his first hole-in-one on this stage....WOW! #Family #memoryofalifetime."

Keegan Bradley, who's played in six Masters, said the Par-3 Contest to him is almost more memorable and enjoyable than the actual tournament. He hadn't played in the Masters for two years before he finally qualified again in 2018.

"[In 2018], I played the Par-3 with my son and my wife," Bradley said. "There have been so many moments at Augusta for me that are like, 'I can't believe this is happening.' And that was one of them. That's truly the only time at any tournament where you really are enjoying it. My first year I played, I played the Par-3 with Phil Mickelson and Ray Floyd. That was so incredible. That I look forward it every year. It's one of the million things that Augusta has mastered."

Paul Azinger calls the Par-3 Contest "one of the greatest additions to any property that I have ever seen in my life."

"That it my favorite place in the world to play golf," Azinger said. "The Par-3 Course at Augusta is peaceful, it's quiet, the greens are unreal and you can make birdies, you can make hole-in-ones. My biggest memory at the Par-3 was Lanny Wadkins fleecing my ass. He taught me how to play Hammer. We were playing $50 a hole Hammer. I said, 'What's Hammer? He said, 'You'll see.' It's the best gambling course I'd seen in my life."

Azinger said the appreciation for the Masters and things like the Par-3 "are so much different now" that he's not competing.

"The Masters means so much to your life," he said. "You didn't know it when you were younger and doing it, but you know it now."

There's no contest about what the most harrowing moment of all the Par-3 Contests has been. That was Tony Finau looking like he'd snapped his ankle in half while celebrating a hole-in-one in 2018.

Finau had just holed out his shot on the seventh hole—"a gap wedge, 121 yards," he said—and he ran off the tee box celebrating, turning back toward his wife and four kids. As he backpedaled, Finau stumbled and was suddenly on the ground with his left foot completely dislocated at the ankle.

"Hole-in-ones are so rare...I think that's why my celebration was so ecstatic," Finau said. "I couldn't believe it. I was so excited I threw the club and just ran toward the hole. People were going nuts. I turned around to see what my family's reaction was and as I was backpedaling, I fell down. There was so much adrenaline, and I didn't know anything had happened.

"It was when I got up that I went, 'Whoa, your foot is laying on the ground right now.' That's when I knew something was wrong. I looked down and just kind of popped the ankle back into place. It was only when I started walking that I was like, 'Oh, something's wrong.'"

When he limped back to the tee, his wife, Alayna, said, "Oh my gosh, dude. Did you really just pop your ankle back in place?"

"That's when I knew the potential was pretty high that the whole world would end up seeing it," Finau said. "I saw where [my foot] was, and I knew where it needed to be. If it didn't work, then I would have laid there and been even more embarrassed being pulled out on a stretcher celebrating a hole-in-one."

The injury looked gruesome and it was a terrifying for Finau, because it was difficult to imagine him being well enough to play the Masters the following day given how had the ankle injury appeared initially.

"He knew there were a lot of people and attention on him and he didn't want to just lay there and call for an ambulance," Finau's caddie, Greg Bodine, said. "So, he just gave it a little nudge and when it popped back in, he said it was a good feeling and the pain went away for a little bit. He's worked his whole life to get here, so for that to happen the day before in such a bright moment...it kind of went from really sweet to really sour."

Finau said he saw the possibility of playing in his first Masters "slipping away."

His anxiety extended over a sleepless night, during which he said "it crossed my mind" that he might have to withdraw from the tournament he'd dreamed about playing in since he was a child. X-rays revealed there were no broken bones, but it wasn't until an MRI at 7:00 AM Thursday that Finau knew there was no significant damage, so he could try to play through the pain without fear of making anything worse.

"We did a lot of praying—just let the kid walk around holy ground one time," Finau's father, Kelepi, said.

"I woke up the next morning and I couldn't put weight on it, and I thought my chances maybe had slipped," Finau said. "But the doctors told me they didn't think I could do any further damage. They said, 'We don't recommend it, but if you're gonna play you're gonna have to tape that thing up.' That's when I decided I'm gonna give it a go, and just told myself, 'No matter what happens, you're gonna finish.'"

Finau not only made his 12:42 PM tee time with his ankle heavily taped, he took a share of the lead in the first round after shooting a 4-under-par 68. (He would go on to finish tied for 10th for the tournament).

"To be in this position I'm at [is] nothing short of a miracle if you ask me," Finau said. "When I woke up this morning, I could barely walk. It was quite crazy, all the emotions that I dealt with overnight, but I was more than ecstatic to just be walking to that first tee and be playing in my first Masters."

Bodine, Finau's caddie, walked off the 18th green with him that afternoon and marveled at what he'd just witnessed.

"The last thing I told him on the 18th green is how much heart he has," Bodine said. "You can't not have heart and play a round like that. He was in pain, but nothing overwhelming. Even if it was, he still would have made it to the first tee. He just wanted to play in the Masters, and I think the cherry on top is that he is competing. We knew if he could swing it, this was possible."

Finau, describing it as "mind over matter," said adrenaline propelled him.

"My story's quite crazy, and I'm sure most of you guys know it by now," the Tongan said of his life that included fire-knife dancing at age four and sleeping in cars at junior tournaments en route to making it to the PGA Tour. "I feel like my back's been up against the wall my whole life, so something like this is just another part of the story, I guess."

Origin

The Par-3 Contest can thank Augusta National Chairman Clifford Roberts for its origin. Initially, Roberts had to work to sway some of the club's members, who thought of it as too hokey, on the idea.

The nine-hole course participants play today is a 1,060-yard par-27 and was designed in 1958 by Roberts and architect George Cobb. The field includes tournament participants, noncompeting past champions, and some other former PGA Tour winners. The holes range from 70 to 140 yards and play over DeSoto Springs

Pond and Ike's Pond. As of 2018, there had been 94 holes-in-one recorded, including nine in 2016—a record.

Sam Snead, who won the Masters in 1949, 1952, and 1954, won the first exhibition in 1960—and would win again in 1974, at age 61. Snead went on to finish 11th in that 1960 Masters, unwittingly beginning the hex that still exists. To this day, only 11 Par-3 winners have ever finished in the top 10 of the Masters Tournament. Through 2018, of the 58 Par-3 Contest winners who played in the Masters the same year, 18 failed to make the cut.

Chapter 8

THE TICKET

Pick the sporting event: Super Bowl, World Series, World Cup soccer, Olympics, College Football Playoff title game, Wimbledon.

No ticket to any of those events comes close in difficulty to procure to a Masters ticket. It's been that way for decades.

Face value for a Masters ticket, if you are fortunate enough to be on the annual patrons list or win the ticket lottery, is $375 for the Thursday through Sunday competition rounds, or $115 per day. They are $75 per day for the Monday through Wednesday practice rounds.

According to Stubhub, in October 2019, a ticket for the 2020 Masters Thursday through Sunday rounds was on sale for $12,500. A ticket for the Monday or Tuesday practice round was selling for $900. A ticket for Wednesday's practice round, the day of the annual Par-3 Contest, was selling for $1,700. Daily tickets for Thursday or Friday were selling for $2,400, and a ticket for the final round on Sunday was going for $7,700.

The secondary market has always been a part of the Masters, though the tournament officials always have frowned upon it, while looking the other way. Recently, though, Augusta National has cracked down on the secondary market, and it's been able to do so with higher technology.

Years ago, the only security that stood between an interloper with no ticket and a walk through the gates and onto the hallowed grounds were a handful of Pinkerton security guards who took only a passing glace at you as you walked in.

Those days before there were photos on the badges and the current sophisticated computer barcode scanners made it easy for someone to either sneak in without a ticket or be assisted in by someone shuffling an extra ticket in, out, and back onto the grounds.

In my early years covering the tournament, I knew someone who would purchase one ticket from a third party and use that one ticket to shuffle some six or eight people onto the grounds.

One year, in the early '90s, that person bought a Masters employee badge for $900 from a ticket broker and used it to shuffle about eight friends into the tournament every day. It was the badge of someone who was supposed to be in charge of restrooms. Clearly, whatever that person got from the ticket broker for his weekly work badge was more than he was getting to clean toilets and sinks for the week.

The ticket broker who sold that employee badge was, and still is, one of the most prominent brokers in the business. He agreed to speak on the condition of anonymity for concern of compromising his business.

"I'm still very active with that event, so I don't know that I want my name used, but I can certainly tell you it's very difficult to procure these tickets," the broker said. "With technology, they're making it more and more and more difficult to get them. It's an extremely, extremely difficult ticket to get, and the reason it's so difficult is that they really don't care. They want their people in, and they don't care about anyone else.

"They want patrons that were on the [waiting] list a long, long time ago. They sell a ham and cheese sandwich for two bucks and the tickets are $375 for the week. I just worked through an event—the U.S. Open tennis—where they charge what the market will bear, and the face value of those tickets was $1,500 for one session. The Masters is $375 for four sessions.

"They've created something that is so special and so unusual where it's not about the money. It's about the experience. I think it's the best-run event in the world. And I'm at every big event that man can imagine—from World Cups to every Olympics since 1992, I've been to every Masters since '88—and there's not an event like this. There just isn't."

There have been a few lines of demarcation at the Masters when the ticket prices have exploded, and Tiger Woods has been involved in most of them.

In 1997, Woods' first Masters, it got so extreme that a prominent local businessman named Allen Caldwell, who'd set up a corporate gathering and promised tickets to all his clients, committed suicide when he realized he'd be unable to deliver the tickets because the cost had spiked too high.

"That was the year Allen Caldwell shot himself under the pressure of trying to get tickets for his event," the ticket broker recalled. "He was a local businessman and very prominent and he sold a lot of his tickets when he didn't realize the tickets that he thought were selling for $2,500 a ticket went up to 10 grand. That was crazy."

Caldwell, 40, was found by his wife in his Augusta home, dead from one shot in the head with a 12-gauge shotgun. He was part-owner of The Clubhouse, an exclusive club across the street from Augusta National Golf Club, where he'd brokered deals to get clients tickets to the tournament.

Caldwell's company, called the Concierge, was in a partnership with World Golf Hospitality of Atlanta, which operated golf packages for corporate clients. At the Clubhouse restaurant, corporations were reported to have leased tables during the Masters for breakfast, lunch, and dinner for $22,000 apiece.

Caldwell apparently sold more tickets to the tournament than he was able to obtain because of the skyrocketing costs, and he couldn't refund money owed to customers who didn't receive their tickets.

Caldwell's club for many years had been a restaurant and bar called the Green Jacket. It was in that parking lot of the Green Jacket where my friend scored that $900 employee restrooms badge, meeting the ticket broker in the back seat of his white stretch limo under the darkness of night.

Security and technology, and more enforcement by Augusta National, are making it more difficult for people—even with money to burn—to find Masters tickets.

In 2018, the Masters started sending letters to patrons whom they'd caught selling their tickets and telling them they were being permanently removed from the yearly ticket list they'd waited so long to get on.

The tournament in 2018 added a new defense to catch sellers of badges—color-coded strips on the bottom of the tickets that tournament officials can use to determine the original purchasers. Each of the colors in the six-color design represents a letter and five numbers that match the corresponding ticket number.

How precious are these annual badges?

People are on waiting lists for years to become regular yearly patrons. And, according to the *Augusta Chronicle*, after a badge holder dies, the account is transferable only to a surviving spouse.

The prominent national ticket broker we interviewed said most of his clients consist of "local patrons that are on the [ticket] list year after year," adding, "Many times, people will rent their house and it comes with four Masters badges at a really inflated price."

"We have a lot of repeat sellers and a lot of repeat buyers, but it's getting more and more difficult and we are trying to get less and less involved," he said. "Most events you want to try to increase your business. This is one event where we're trying to decrease the business. [Masters officials] are asking patrons questions about where they got the tickets. It's getting to the point where, in my opinion, they're pushing the envelope. They know very well what is happening, that buying and re-selling these tickets is taking place.

"If they crack down and upset the wrong people, meaning a lot of very important clients who are there, they're thrown out. And what you don't want to do is ruin the system, because the system is working. They don't want to get too good at this cracking down on the re-selling, because then pretty soon the people they want to attract aren't coming."

Chapter 9

BUTLER CABIN

B utler Cabin seems like a mythical place. Few know where it actually is. Fewer know its origin and what or whom it's named after. But almost every golf fan has heard of it.

For all his prolific accomplishments in broadcasting, including being the lead NFL play-by-play person for CBS, the network's top NCAA Tournament voice, and so many other things, broadcaster Jim Nantz is probably known more for his broadcasts from the Masters—and specifically Butler Cabin—than for anything else.

Sometime around 8:00 at night on the final-round Sunday of every Masters, tens of millions of television viewers watch the Masters winner have the coveted green jacket slipped over his shoulders by the defending champion.

Directly after winning the tournament, the player who wins the Masters is whisked off to the cabin, where he will be interviewed for the first time as the champion by Nantz, who asks the first questions of the latest green jacket winner.

The annual ritual takes place in the lower floor of a white house located just off the main clubhouse at Augusta National Golf Club called Butler Cabin.

Only the privileged ever have entered Butler Cabin.

The overwhelming majority of players who have competed in the Masters—even those who have played more than a decade in the tournament—have never been inside Butler Cabin. Not unless they have won a green jacket. Some players don't even know exactly where it is located.

It took me until the 21st Masters I'd covered for the *New York Post* before I not only entered Butler Cabin but even knew where it was located. I was invited in by Nantz on the eve of the 2014 Masters.

My curiosity was piqued during a conversation I had with Adam Scott, the 2013 Masters winner. When I asked what the most memorable moment was in the immediate aftermath of his victory the year before, the first thing Scott referenced was Butler Cabin.

"I have a lot of memories—some are a blur—but standing in Butler Cabin was most memorable, because I'd been going to the Masters for 11 years and I'd never even been there before," Scott said. "So when I was standing in that room under the portrait of Bobby Jones with the chairman of the club and Jim Nantz, it was that spot that we always watch on TV. It was something I'd never seen live before, only on TV."

Scott's description of Butler Cabin sounded like someone describing a trip to a back lot of studios in Hollywood and see-ing the façade of the house from *The Munsters* or *The Addams Family*.

"The room is pretty much a backdrop," Scott said. "I just remember a lot of television cameras and production people on the other side of the room. The whole thing is very staged."

What the other 51 weeks of the year is a living room with a big flat screen TV on the wall for club members and their guests who stay in the cabin is transformed into a high-tech

TV studio, with monitors and sound equipment everywhere and multiple cameras pointed toward those wooden chairs in front of a fireplace with a portrait of club founder Bobby Jones above it.

Nantz, the voice of the Masters since 1988, has been a part of and witnessed so many memorable moments inside that cabin. Lives have changed inside that room. Dreams have become reality.

"I often look down at the carpet right here and think about the people who have actually stood on this very spot through history—Jack [Nicklaus], Arnie [Palmer], Gary Player, Tiger [Woods], Phil's [Mickelson's] coronation—it all happened right here," Nantz said.

When Nantz was a college student—and roommate of Fred Couples—at the University of Houston, he used to rehearse the Butler Cabin ceremony, pretending he was the host.

So, when Couples won the green jacket in 1992, it presented Nantz with one of the most challenging dilemmas of his career. How was he possibly going to hold it together emotionally on the air when he and Couples were realizing their dreams together on national television?

"It was the hardest single thing I've ever had to do in broadcasting, because I was so personally tied to the moment and I knew I had a professional responsibility to conduct an interview as if he was just another player," Nantz recalled. "But he wasn't just another player. He was a guy I lived with in college and one of my closest friends. I walked out of there that day and felt I had grown as a broadcaster. I had taken on a really potentially difficult situation and had it come off the way it should have.

"Who could ever top that moment unless the presenter was the father and the champion was the son? He always wanted to be the Masters champion and I always wanted to broadcast the Masters for CBS. The fact that the two of us had aspirations that would bring us to this one room...what are the odds?"

Couples fondly recalled that special moment.

"I remember being awfully nervous playing and winning, and then being more nervous going in there, because it's a spot you're never really used to going," Couples said of his Butler Cabin visit with his old pal, Nantz.

"That's the happiest moment of my career, seeing my buddy win the green jacket like we rehearsed," Nantz said.

Most of the time, it is the Masters winner who's holding back the tears. On that occasion, it was both Nantz and Couples.

"I could barely get the words out," Nantz said. "My voice was quivering."

Couples best encapsulated Butler Cabin when he once said, "It's the only spot to be in Augusta on Sunday night."

One of the greatest gifts associated with his position as the Butler Cabin host for those green jacket ceremonies is Nantz always can feel the weight of the moment for the winner.

"It's a big moment in their lifetimes," Nantz said. "For a lot of them, it's a coronation being in that room."

Earlier that week, Nantz taped a Masters special with past champions Nick Faldo, Bernhard Langer, and José María Olazábal, and they did it inside Butler Cabin in those wooden chairs— something that, because of where they sat, carried emotional significance.

"They all waxed about the gravity of that moment in this room," Nantz said. "They had not been back in the room since they presented the jacket as defending champion."

Until he began working for CBS in 2008, Faldo had not been back to the cabin since the night when, as the defending

1996 champion, he slipped the green jacket over the shoulders of Tiger Woods in 1997.

"The first time he came into the cabin for CBS, he sat down in the chair across from me and he had tears in his eyes," Nantz said.

"I get emotional every time I walk in there now, because I realize that very simple path between those two doors—the front door and the one to the actual room—is one of the shortest, most significant walks in sport," Faldo said. "It's only about five paces and you're in, and that means you're the champion, which is amazing."

Faldo, who's won three Masters, called the trip to Butler Cabin after a win "a blur," because the winner is whisked from the 18th green to the cabin so the TV broadcast can go off on time. And in Faldo's case, he won two of his three Masters in a playoff.

"You can imagine, two of those you've walked off a playoff and you're in there two minutes later," Faldo said. "You're dealing with that, first time you've won, you're in a playoff, the emotion of the Greg [Norman] battle, you're not yourself in there. You go into silent mode. It's not the place to start chatting away."

Faldo is in a unique position as someone who's visited Butler Cabin as a player and now as a broadcaster, working with Nantz at CBS.

"The first time I went in there, my very first year at CBS, I suddenly realized I hadn't been back there since I was a player," Faldo said. "You don't recognize it. There's cameras and wires running, there's technicians. You don't even notice it in those days [as a player]. Now it's a studio."

Oftentimes, the player who's just won the Masters and arrives to Butler Cabin for the made-for-TV ceremony gets an added bonus of having the green jacket slipped on by the defending champion.

Tommy Aaron, the 1973 Masters winner, recalled in a story in the *Augusta Chronicle* being thrilled that Jack Nicklaus, the 1972 winner, was going to do the honors. "It's very special to have the best player in the game put the coat on you," Aaron said.

There are rare times when the defending champion wins again, as was the case when Tiger Woods won in 2001 and 2002. There was no other defending champion to put Woods' jacket on.

There have been a fair share of awkward moments inside the cabin, too, like Woods giving the green jacket to his rival Phil Mickelson and Jordan Spieth giving it to Danny Willet minutes after throwing away the tournament himself, losing a five-shot lead on the back nine.

Nantz said, when he comes across people curious about Butler Cabin, "people are very thrown off by what it is. They think it might be the butler's cabin, where people who work for the club live."

It actually is a cabin that once belonged to Thomas Baldwin Butler of Baltimore, who was a member of Augusta National and played golf with his friend, Dwight Eisenhower, the former president, who also has a cabin named after him.

Butler cabin is one of 10 cabins on the grounds of Augusta National. While seven of the 10 cabins form a semicircle east of the tenth fairway and west of the Par-3 Course, the Eisenhower, Butler, and Roberts Cabins stand alone. Butler Cabin is situated between the clubhouse and the Par-3 Course, just behind the practice putting green and 10th tee box. It was built in 1964 and CBS first started using it in 1965.

"There is not a day that goes by that I don't get asked about Augusta and the Butler Cabin—by athletes, coaches, walking through airports," Nantz said. "It comes up in my life every day."

PART FOUR

THURSDAY

Chapter 10

THE RESTAURANT

The 19th hole at the Masters isn't even located on the grounds of Augusta National.

TBonz Steakhouse, located a long par-5 down Washington Road from the club, is the unofficial Masters 19th hole. It also happens to be the most difficult dinner table to book in Augusta during tournament week. Scoring a table for four there is about as difficult as getting a foursome onto Augusta National.

The restaurant is a lot of things to Masters week, beginning with Augusta's most iconic gathering place for fans to rub elbows with the who's who in the world of golf over icy beers and sizzling steaks.

It, too, is the unofficial caddie headquarters, with caddies making up a lot of the clientele. The caddie for the Masters winner each year traditionally has a party there—and picks up the tab. Current and former players mingle, as do their agents, coaches, media, and big hitters in the golf business.

"Masters week is our Super Bowl here, in this restaurant," TBonz owner Mark Cumins said.

Cumins estimates that TBonz does five weeks' worth of business during the seven days in Augusta during Masters week.

Some 6,000 pounds of beef—three tons—are ordered for Masters week. The restaurant averages about 1,000 covers a day during Masters week.

"These people, if they're hungry, they'll sit in a plant if we'll seat them there," Cumins said.

Cumins, a Willie Nelson doppelganger with his long (sometimes pony-tailed) gray locks and facial scruff, has owned TBonz since he and his partner, Jerry Scheer, opened it in 1986. TBonz is the first of 25 restaurants Cumins opened and owns in South Carolina, North Carolina, and Georgia.

"One partner and three wives," Cumins joked. "I'm on my third wife."

Cumins, who lives in Charleston, South Carolina, where some of his other restaurants are located, said he comes to Augusta about four times a year for more than one day, and spends 10 to 12 days there before, during and after Masters week.

Cumins and TBonz are as much the soul of Masters week as anything you'll find there. They are as much a fabric of those seven days in Augusta as the signature azaleas around Augusta National. Those who have become regulars over the years come to see and spend time with Cumins as much as they come for the steaks and drinks.

Cumins, an Augusta native who got his college degree in special education at the University of Georgia and had plans to pursue that as a career, said he had "no idea" he'd end up a prolific restauranteur and certainly less of an idea that he'd become such a significant part of Masters week.

"We were just hard-working guys that, the harder we worked, the luckier we got," Cumins said. "We didn't have any money when we started. We just had good ideas. I never even meant to be in this business all my life. After about 15 or 20 years here, I really felt like we'd be here forever."

Cumins' charm is as much his humble nature as his ability to connect with all walks of life.

"If I say this place is iconic, I almost feel like that gives me an ego, and I don't have an ego," Cumins said. "I always tell people that all I care is that you walk out with a smile on your face. If you do, you're going to come back."

And they do. The people come back in droves. That includes some celebrity folks who've become some of Cumins' closest friends. Darius Rucker, the face of the band Hootie and the Blowfish, is one of Cumins' best friends and a regular at TBonz during Masters week. Former Kansas City Royals third baseman and Hall of Famer George Brett is another member of Cumins' inner circle.

And on it goes.

"One thing about Masters week: everybody is somebody," Cumins said. "Some of them, just ask them and they'll tell you. Most of them won't, because they really are somebody."

For example...

"Admiral Mike Mullen, the former chairman of the Joint Chiefs of Staff, he's here every Friday night of Masters week," Cumins said. "It's the only time all week I sit down and have dinner here. We sit at that table right over there. This guy was the third most hated guy in the world, stood behind Obama when they took out Bin Laden. He comes right here. Sits right back at that table. He's the nicest guy. You wouldn't know who he was."

Cumins' father, Jerry, was from the Bronx and his mother from Brooklyn. His older sisters were born in New York.

"My mom used to tell the story about my dad taking his Jewish family from New York to Augusta," Cumins said. "When they landed at Bush Field in Augusta, she said, 'Jerry, what have you done to me?' She said there were people in lawn chairs sitting around watching the planes land. That's the way Augusta was, a small town."

Jerry Cumins died at age 48 in 1972 when Mark was 15.

The first restaurant Cumins worked at as a teenager was a place called Steak and Egg Kitchen, where he was a short-order cook.

"I always worked at least one or two jobs while I was in school, and I worked for some really good chefs in Athens, Georgia," he recalled. "I always say I went to school of hard knocks to be a chef, because back then the chefs would throw a pan or knife at you. They were some fiery dudes. They thought they walked on water and whatever they said went and if you didn't listen to them you were going to get rapped upside the head with something."

Now, years later and with 25 restaurants, Cumins is more of an overseer of his operations than a hands-on owner.

"At this point, I'm a schmoozer," he said. "One of the things I do is I connect. I like connecting. I think people connect back, especially if you give them the time to talk and you listen to them. It doesn't matter who you are or what you do in life. Rush Limbaugh is one of my closest friends. George Brett is one of my closest friends. I've traveled the world with these guys and played golf with them.

"I'm a poor Jew from Augusta. What am I doing flying in these people's planes? It's all the connections."

He estimates he's played Augusta National about 15 times.

"I have some member friends there," he said. "I played it a few times growing up in high school. It was always super special to play out there. But now it's ridiculous what hoops people will jump though to play it."

Cumins grows emotional when he talks about Masters week as it relates to his late father.

"My only regret is that he never got to see me have success," Cumins said, wiping tears from his eyes. "My dad used to take me out there to the National, I remember holding his leg and rolling down the hills on the grass, that's what I think about Masters week. When I see a dad and a son here at the restaurant, I say, 'Son, remember this. Dad, remember this. Because this is your time. This is such a great father-son opportunity.'

"I remember holding my dad's leg when I was 4, 5, 6 years old and he would let me go and I would roll down the hill by No. 18 and No. 9. Back then, you could do that. I did it with my kids when they were little, because that was my memory. I remember sitting on my dad's shoulders and seeing fat Jack [Nicklaus] when he first came with that flat-top crew cut he had, and Arnold Palmer...I remember all those guys.

"I was right there [in 1968] when Roberto De Vicenzo came out of the tent after he'd signed the scorecard wrong [to lose the Masters]. He was blubbering like a baby and they had a cart waiting for him to take him back up to the clubhouse and his head was buried in his hands."

Two incredible things happened in 1987, which was the first Masters during which TBonz was open.

The first was a kismet meeting with Fred Couples at the restaurant. Couples came for dinner with his then-caddie, Joe LaCava, on the Monday night of 1987 Masters week.

"The next day I'm on the course, just kind of walking around and relaxing and I'm on the ninth fairway crosswalk and Freddie was on the other side of the fairway," Cumins recalled. "I'm standing there and there were a lot of people around and Joe points over to me, telling Freddie, 'That's the guy from last night at TBonz.'

"Freddie hits his shot onto the green and walks all the way over to me with Joe and all people see this and start walking over. And Freddie says, 'Hey Mark, how are you doing? I had a great meal at your restaurant last night. Your steaks are awesome, and I'm coming back tonight. Can you get me a table around 7 o'clock for eight of us?'

"I said, 'Yes sir, absolutely.' He winked and walked away. So, all these people are now asking me, 'What place was he talking about and where is it?' That night a lot of people came. It was like a springboard for business. Freddie must have told some players, too, and some other caddies about it, because in comes Peter Jacobson, Scott Hoch, Mark O'Meara, David Frost, and all these players. What he said and how he said it just blew me away, because he didn't have to do that.

"The coolest guy. The sun don't set on a cool motherfucker like that, I'm telling you."

Cumins said he used to ask Couples to put his TBonz T-shirts in the lockers of some players for them to sign.

"He would get it done for me and I have them framed on the wall of the restaurant," Cumins said. "Freddie won the Masters in '92. I sent a bottle of Dom to him, and the next morning he showed up with the shirts because he didn't forget. But he said, 'I'm not going to be in that locker room anymore. I'm going to be in the Champions Locker Room.'"

The other unforgettable moment in that 1987 Masters was the fact that Larry Mize won the green jacket. Mize is an Augusta native whom Cumins knew growing up.

"Our first Masters at the restaurant was when Larry Mize won, which was unbelievable," Cumins said. "I played a little golf when I was younger, and Larry Mize played for Augusta Prep. My buddies and I would all play golf, go swimming, play tennis, and chase girls. And Larry would be on the back of the driving range hitting 1,000 balls practicing. He was such a nice guy, but we would all go, 'What does he think, that he's going to win the Masters some year?' "

Chapter 11

TIGER, 1997

N o one had any idea what was about to unfold in the 1997 Masters.

Who could have predicted the history to which the golf world would be treated?

Who could have predicted that the '97 Masters would become the gateway to the greatest two-decade run of golf in the sport?

Tiger Woods was an idea in 1997. People in the sport had heard of him, were aware of his remarkable amateur career. He'd arrived as a pro with that aggressive, eye-opening, if gaudy, "I am Tiger Woods" Nike commercial campaign that took overt digs at the elitist and racist establishment about the clubs he could not get into because of the color of his skin.

But no one—probably not even Tiger Woods himself—could have predicted what would happen at the 1997 Masters and the two decades that would follow, with 14 more major championships and 82 wins after that historic, memorable week at Augusta National.

Surely, there was a curiosity about how Woods would fare as a professional. That '97 Masters was his first as a professional. He'd played twice as an amateur (in 1995 and '96), with the

101

winner and runner-up of the U.S. Amateur gaining an invite to the Masters.

So, when Woods made the turn in 4-over par-40 in his Thursday opening round, there was an understandable feeling about the grounds that maybe it was too much too soon for the 21-year-old kid, regardless of his otherworldly, God-given talent.

What would happen for the next 63 holes was dizzying. Woods torched one of the world's best and most treacherous golf courses and the world-class field and won the tournament in a runaway, shattering records along the way and shocking everyone in attendance.

"I have to confess, part of you goes, 'He's not living up to the hype,'" English golfer Paul Casey recalled about seeing that slow Thursday start by Woods.

Casey, who has become an accomplished professional with multiple wins and Ryder Cup appearances, was still in school at Arizona State and watching it all on TV when Woods was doing what he did in '97 at Augusta.

"You jump straight on in and say, 'He shot 40 on the front nine, he's never going to come back,'" Casey said. "That's what makes that win more amazing. You've just got to bow down and go, 'What was that all about?'"

By the time the week was over, Woods had obliterated records at Augusta. At 21, he became the youngest winner, two years younger than 1980 champion Seve Ballesteros.

His 72-hole score of 270 is the lowest ever, one shot better than Jack Nicklaus in 1965 and Raymond Floyd in 1976.

His 12-shot margin of victory over Tom Kite is a record.

Does anyone remember that Kite finished runner-up in that '97 Masters?

"It was nice to be in the hunt even though nobody was really in the hunt," Kite said that day. "We were after the silver medal."

Woods played 72 holes without a single three-putt green, which is an accomplishment at a place where the greens are more difficult to putt than any in the world.

Nicklaus, the record six-time Masters winner, famously said on the day Woods was winning his first of five green jackets, "Tiger is out there playing another game. He's playing a game we're not familiar with. If he's playing well, the golf course becomes nothing. With his power, he's making this golf course melt away. He's playing a golf course he'll own for a long time. This young man will win many more. It's not my time anymore. It's his."

Nicklaus had seen greatness in Woods after playing with him in the previous year's Masters and related a conversation he had with Arnold Palmer after that.

"Arnold and I both agree that you could take his Masters and my Masters and add them together, and this kid should win more than that," Nicklaus said, referring to the combined 10 green jackets he and Palmer won. "This kid is the most fundamentally sound golfer I've ever seen at almost any age."

Tom Watson, a three-time Masters winner who finished fourth in 1997, called Woods "a boy among men, and he's showing the men how to play."

Andy North, a two-time U.S. Open champion who played in 13 Masters and, as an ESPN analyst has called many more of them, hadn't seen anyone overwhelm Augusta the way Woods did since Nicklaus.

"He changed so many things in the game in much the same way that we saw Arnold [Palmer] do it back in the late '50s and early '60s. The television contracts exploded."

Stuart Appleby, an Australian golfer who came close a couple times to winning a Masters but never crossed the line, called Woods' win as it related to the sport "a turning point at Augusta."

"I think the members just went, 'Man, this course is too easy,'" Appleby said. "That's when the changes started. Augusta was made obsolete. The course was too short for him."

What followed was a series of changes to the golf course—adding length and planting more trees. Those were projects that were unofficially termed "Tiger-proofing." Augusta measured 6,925 yards from the tournament tees in 1997. In 2019, it played longer than 7,400 yards.

"I will never forget the way he played the 18th hole," Ernie Els recalled. "He made it look like a chip-and-putt course. We were hitting eight-irons. He hit a drive around the corner. The flag was in the back right and he hit a sand wedge, which went over the green, took a back spin, and almost went in the hole. It was stuff that nobody could do in those days."

Back then, Woods was the most prolific driver of the golf ball the game had ever seen. That week at Augusta in 1997, Woods led the 86-man field in average driving distance at 323 yards. He was 25 yards longer on average than the next player, Scott McCarron.

"Tiger completely overpowered the par-5s at Augusta," Adam Scott, the 2012 Masters winner, said. "I remember how on each of the first two days he hit a wedge for his second shot into the 500-yard, par-5 15th hole. He kept going at the pins."

Bernhard Langer won the Masters in 1985 and 1993. So he knew his way around Augusta National about as well as anyone walking the grounds. And yet...

"I couldn't believe some of the clubs he was hitting," Langer said. "He was demolishing some of the par-4s and par-5s. It was sort of unheard of at the time. That got the Masters to do something about that—plant trees and make it longer. At that time, it looked like he was going to break Jack's record and be the greatest player ever. Then he took a different turn."

Nick Price recalled Woods "totally overpowered the golf course," adding, "We had not seen that happen at Augusta, I think, probably since Nicklaus back in the '60s. It was a clinic for all of us. We knew that this was a whole new ballgame now."

Ben Crenshaw, who won the Masters twice, the second time two years before Woods' '97 win, said the day Woods won, "I've always thought a lot of things happen here for a reason."

Memories

Everyone associated with the game—players, media, fans—has his or her own memory of what went down that week in 1997 and what it meant to them.

"Watching it, you could see and feel it was important," Spanish golfer and 2017 Masters winner Sergio García said. "It wasn't something normal. The next day was a Monday and I remember talking about it with my friends in school."

It remains one of those rare events where you can still remember where you were and what you were doing when it happened.

Charles Howell III is an Augusta native who used to play high school matches at Augusta National and went to every Masters as a youth. He said he "had known of" Woods before that week and "knew he was special, but I don't think anybody quite knew he was all that."

"In that win that week, he checked all the boxes," Howell said. "He's young, he hit it far, he hit it straight, he had a phenomenal short game. He did it all, and he did it on the biggest, hardest stage in the world. I think in the history of time we'll look back on that week as sort of a turning point for the professional game."

Els, who in later years would become a frequent major championship bridesmaid to Woods, said he remembered seeing Woods on the range after that roller-coaster opening-round 70 that began with the 40 on the front nine and ended with a 30 on the back, "and I could see the excitement and the joy" in Woods' face.

"He knew he'd won the first hurdle," Els said. "I think he knew then that it was over."

Nick Faldo, the defending champion who was paired with Woods in that opening round, knew it was over, too.

"The way I analyzed it, he went out in 40, came back in 30 and we didn't see him for dust for another 14 years," Faldo said. "That was the start of Tiger and the start of his dominance. It was a special day. You go out in 40 and then you win by 12. That's something pretty unique."

Faldo shot 75 that day and followed it with an 81 and missed the cut.

Paul Azinger, an 11-time PGA Tour winner with one major championship and now a TV analyst for NBC and FOX, was paired with Woods in the second round. He began the day one shot ahead of Woods and ended it six shots behind after Woods' 66 to his 73.

"I'd never seen Tiger actually make a full swing and hit a shot—driving range, golf course, nothing—maybe on TV," Azinger recalled. "I said to my caddie on the second hole—there was a little bit of a wait—and I said, 'You know, I've never seen this kid hit a shot. I'm going to watch this.' I'd heard about how far he hits it. That ball left four feet underneath the top of the trees, which is miles high, never curved an inch, about five feet right of the trees.

"It was the most beautiful, picturesque drive I had ever seen in my entire life. I just looked at my caddie and whispered to him, 'Holy shit.' That was all I could say. He hit 6- or 7-iron in there to the right of the green, was all ticked off, chunked his chip, took the club and slammed it in the bag, and it went straight to the bottom. It sounded like a drum. I can remember this buzz of the crowd. It was the most unique buzz. He then chipped in for birdie. He shot the easiest 66 that I'd ever seen.

"I hit 3-wood, 8-iron to 13 and he hit 3-wood pitching wedge. I hit driver, 8-iron into 15, he hit driver, pitching wedge. We were two clubs apart, which blew my mind that I was two clubs shorter than anybody on Tour. I was like, 'Really? Two clubs? Are you kidding me?' One club is one thing, two clubs? You can't defend against being two clubs shorter than somebody. You're not going to beat that guy.

"It intimidated me a little bit. That's why I tried not to hit balls near Tiger on the practice range, because I wanted to feed my confidence."

Azinger said after that second round he'd played with Woods, he thought, "I don't know how anybody's going to beat that."

"I didn't jump the gun and predict he would win," Azinger said. "But in my head, I was thinking, 'Jack [Nicklaus] was right saying that he's going to win the Masters 10 times.' I believe him. The bigger the event, the higher he'll raise the bar. He's Michael Jordan in long pants."

One of the great exchanges of that week involved Colin Montgomerie, the sometimes prickly Scotsman who was paired with Woods in Saturday's third round.

On Friday night, Montgomerie, who was three shots behind Woods at the time, waxed poetic about the fact that the young Woods had never been in the position of taking a major championship lead into the weekend and how everything changes on the weekend of a major.

"The pressure is mounting," Montgomerie said in what clearly was a public warning to Woods. "And I have a lot more experience in major championships."

Woods, in his book *The 1997 Masters: My Story*, revealed that Montgomerie's words "definitely motivated me."

Woods shot 65 that Saturday to Montgomerie's 74, and after the round, Montgomerie spoke as if he had seen a ghost.

"All I have to say is one brief comment today," he told reporters. "There is no chance...we're all human beings here...[and] there is no chance humanly possible that Tiger is going to lose this tournament. No way."

Montgomerie recalled that Saturday round by Woods as "the easiest 65 I've ever seen."

"From the second hole onwards, I thought, 'Hang on a minute. This is something extraordinary,'" Montgomerie said. "This is a game that I had not seen before and none of us had. I'm probably the reason he did what he did. I thought I would beat him. I was wrong. But I admitted it.

"I'd just witnessed something very special. I thought I shot a very solid 74 until I lost to him by nine shots. I witnessed something that nobody else had seen."

Montgomerie, surely rattled by the thumping he took from Woods on Saturday, shot 81 on Sunday.

Woods, asked after his round on the Saturday if he'd thought about the accomplishment winning the Masters would be, said, "It would mean a lot, for a number of reasons. I'll be the youngest to win. I think it will open up a lot of doors, a lot of opportunities, and draw a lot of people into golf who never thought of playing the game. It's going to do a lot for the game, as far as minority golf is concerned."

Nicklaus had zero doubt about what the outcome would be the next day.

"I think everybody can go home right now," Nicklaus said. "He's in a trance."

Italian Costantino Rocca was paired with Woods in the final round. Trailing by eight shots at the start, Rocca played a bit part in the coronation as Woods shot 69 and won by a record 12 shots.

"At that time, he was very powerful and the people were going crazy to see this thing," Rocca recalled. "From the 13th to the 18th, the people supported him like crazy. I don't know if anyone remembered I was on the golf course. It was good for him, not for me."

Stricker had just played with Woods earlier in the year at Pebble Beach and realized, "I don't have that game."

"He's playing it 310 or 315 [yards off the tee] and hitting 3-wood past my driver and he just had this intimidating look about him and this belief in himself," Stricker said. "So, I saw it earlier in the year. But then to see him put it all together at Augusta was pretty cool. He showed the world what he was capable of at that time...and it was just a glimpse of what was to come."

Gary Woodland, the 2019 U.S. Open champion, as a teenage boy living in Kansas and playing every sport he could in '97, said he watched that '97 Masters on a VHS tape his mother gave him, and it changed his life.

"I watched it over and over and that's when I got excited about golf," Woodland said. "I was playing so many other sports that I wasn't focused on golf. But Tiger was an athlete. Where I grew up, nobody played golf. But he made it cool.

"That week changed everything for me. I probably would have tried to play baseball or something else, but he made it cool for athletes to play golf and that's what I wanted to do. Eventually, I probably will tell him that."

Brendan Steele was also an impressionable teenager back then, growing up outside of Palm Springs, California, when Woods did what he did in '97.

"I had just kind of picked up golf," Steele said. "I definitely remember sitting around and watching that Masters and being so blown away by it—the dominance and the madness. I don't know that I would be where I am without that week. It definitely motivated me and excited me about the game more than I had ever been before."

Tony Finau recalled that the first golf tournament he ever watched was the '97 Masters, and he said, "Just watching Tiger dominate the way that he did was very inspiring for me for some reason as a kid, and I took up the game the summer of '97, I think in huge part because of Tiger. Tiger is a huge, huge inspiration and influence on me, and that '97 Masters meant a lot."

Jordan Spieth, the 2016 Masters winner, said, "There's nobody who had more influence in my golf game than Tiger."

"He brought it in every tournament...the dominance, the way that he was able to bring it in the majors, the way that he was able to kind of get into contention and be in contention and be at that highest kind of mental part of the game week-in and week-out and major-in and major-out."

Jason Day was a nine-year-old living in Rockhampton, a town in rural Queensland, Australia, when Woods was changing the game in a week.

"My dad had this turn-knob TV with bunny ears, and you had to move the antenna to get the right picture and it was like really early in the morning," Day recalled. "I remember [Woods] walking up the 18th and he obliterated the field. There's two moments where Tiger really got me into golf—that moment when he won the '97 Masters and I started playing more golf than I usually did at that age. Then when I read a book about him when I was 14. Those are the two moments that really kind of changed my life with regards to my career."

Ian Poulter, who was manning his local pro shop in England, selling golf shirts, when Woods was dismantling Augusta in '97, said what transpired "opened everyone's eyes."

"When that happened in '97, you don't think anything other than, 'Wow, this kid's exceptional,'" Poulter said. "But I don't think anyone thought right then he's going to win 15 majors and take on Jack's record."

North was working his first Masters as an analyst at ESPN that year and called Woods' dominance "a signal that the rest of the golf world was going to be in a lot of trouble if they expected to beat this guy."

"And then there was the impact he's had over the last 20 years," North said. "He made golf cool for a lot of younger kids. If you were a kid playing in high school golf team back in the late '90s and early 2000s all of a sudden now you were proud to walk through the front door of the school with your golf clubs to put in your locker, versus trying to sneak them in the back door. Now, all of a sudden people recognized that golf was a sport that meant something."

Other than that second round in which he played with Woods, Azinger's lasting memory was what Augusta National looked like when the tournament ended.

"When he went out on Sunday and Lee Elder [the first black golfer to play in the Masters] was out there, you realized that this was bigger than anything golf had ever seen," Azinger said. "And then it played out to be that way. All the employees from the clubhouse came out. It was just a gigantic cultural moment. He just reached way beyond golf. Way beyond it. He was bigger in Asia than he was in the United States, as big as he was here.

"Suddenly, you realized this was a global brand, and Nike helped build it. But you can't become a global brand unless you can perform. Nobody could ever have seen Tiger Woods coming. Nobody could see it, and they'd be lying if they said they could."

There was some symbolism to Woods winning in front of Elder. Woods was born in 1975, the year Elder broke the color barrior at the Masters.

Two months after that Masters win, Woods took over the world No. 1 ranking for the first time. He stayed there for only a week, but over the next 17 years he would stay atop the rankings more often than not. Woods holds the record for the longest consecutive period of time ranked No. 1, at 683 weeks, more than double Greg Norman's previous record of 331 weeks.

Historic Moment

Woods put on the green jacket for that 1997 Masters and received a congratulatory phone call from president Bill Clinton. Two days later, he would appear at Shea Stadium to mark the 50th anniversary of Jackie Robinson's major league debut. At age 21, he was transcending the sport of golf.

As Woods made the turn on Sunday, nine holes from making history, he remembered what his father, Earl, had told him the night before.

"He said it would probably be the toughest round I would ever play, but to be myself and it would be the most rewarding round I ever played," Woods recalled.

When Woods walked up the 18th fairway, he said he thought about golfers such as Elder and other trailblazers like Charlie Sifford, with whom he would later forge a close relationship.

"I wasn't the pioneer," Woods said after winning. "Charlie Sifford, Lee Elder, Ted Rhodes, those are the guys who paved the way. Coming up 18, I said a little prayer of thanks to those guys. Those guys are the ones who did it. I thank them. If it wasn't for them, I might not have had the chance to play here."

When his final putt disappeared into the cup, Woods hugged his parents at the side of the 18th green and wept as he embraced Earl, who whispered in his son's ear, "We did it. I love you and I'm so proud. Now let it all out."

A short time later, at the awards ceremony, Wood said, "I've always dreamed of playing the Masters and winning it. Everyone who is a little kid dreams of playing in the Masters and winning it, and I was able to do that. It means a lot to myself and my family and anyone who knows how much I always wanted to win this tournament. I never thought I would have the lead like I did. It's not what you envision. You envision dueling it out with, I guess, Faldo or Nicklaus or Watson, someone who's awfully tough to beat down the stretch.

"You dream of that, or getting into a playoff, weird things like that. But never to do it in the fashion I did. That's just something you never really dream of. It's just kind of nice that it actually became a reality."

Earl Woods, at the sight of his son wearing the green jacket, said, "Green and black go well together, don't they?"

Elder had made the trip up from his home in Florida to Augusta to witness the Woods coronation.

That Sunday's final round came two days before the 50th anniversary of Jackie Robinson breaking baseball's color barrier was not lost on Earl Woods, Lee Elder, or anyone else.

"I'm sure Jackie Robinson would've been extremely proud of Tiger," Earl Woods said.

"I'm so proud," Elder said. "We have a black champion. That's going to have major significance. It will open the door for more blacks to become members here. It will get more minority kids involved in golf."

————

Game Changer

Outside of the exclusive gates of Augusta National, there were seismic shifts in the game as a result of Woods' explosion onto the scene, highlighted by that '97 Masters victory. The television money became massive and tournament purses became exponentially larger.

According to the PGA Tour, total prize money in 1997 was $80,550,000. As of 2020, it's pushing $300 million.

In short, Woods' success, and the hysteria that followed, has helped line fellow players' pockets. It's made the people who run the PGA Tour millionaires. And it all started with that 1997 Masters victory.

"I can't think of one golf tournament that's changed the game more than that one," Charles Howell III said. "You can almost pinpoint to that week the reason we're playing for the money we're playing for today and the fanfare of the game."

Ian Poulter said, "That week changed everything. It changed golf for everybody. It changed courses for us all, it changed purses, it changed equipment."

Adam Scott recalled watching the tournament at home in Australia having no idea how it was about to change the entire landscape of the sport.

"It was the start of something amazing that happened over the next 10 or 11 years," Scott said. "If you think just about the reaction to how he played that golf course and then now what Augusta National Golf Club looks like now compared to what it looked like for the 50 years before Tiger, that's a significant change.

"And then, you think of the influence Augusta National Golf Club has over golf around the rest of the world and the way courses have since been treated. They kind of led the Tiger-proofing, and now it seems like every course is Tiger-proofed."

Life was moving fast for Woods at the time. So fast that not even he could see or understand the magnitude of his own accomplishments or the effect he was having on the sport he was about to dominate for the better part of next two decades.

"I guess when you're in the well, it's hard to see what's going on outside of it," Woods said in 2019. "The perspective I got over the years, of people talking about how much it meant to them, I never knew that. I was out there trying to get my own green jacket."

Woods' performance at the '97 Masters changed the landscape of the sport. He changed the game of golf for the better—for everyone, drawing a new young generation of players to the game, making players wealthier than they ever dreamed they'd be. He raised the bar for performance so high he forced everyone to be better.

"All these great players you see now playing golf, around the world and in [the Masters] tournament, they came from sitting at home watching Tiger Woods play golf," Lance Barrow, the producer on the CBS telecast every year since 1997, said. "They all said, 'Hey, we can do that.' You see their swagger, the way they play, their go-for-broke attitude. At every golf tournament now, including the Masters, there are 20 people within one or two shots of the lead because they all watched Tiger growing up and they all said, 'You know, I can play like that.'"

Chapter 12

THE PATRON

When he first hatched the idea of going to Augusta National as a fan in 2000, Oliver Katcher never thought it would turn into this.

There is no official title for what Katcher does or has done over the course of the 19 Masters he has attended through 2019, but he's definitely become an unofficial "superfan" of sorts.

The 48-year-old New York City native who works in commercial real estate does have a description of what he does.

"I'm one of the best in the world at going to the Masters, not playing the Masters," Katcher said.

You'd have to look far and wide to find a fan who's more dialed in to the Masters experience than Katcher, who has his routines—some brilliantly clever, some borderline militant, and some downright quirky.

Among the most beautifully quirky is Katcher's routine from Saturday to Sunday.

He never attends the final round on Sunday. On Saturday afternoon, Katcher buys upward of 100 sandwiches—the famous pimento cheese, the Masters clubs, the chicken breast, egg salad, and chicken salad—brings them back to New York City, and has an intimate gathering at his Manhattan apartment, where he and his guests watch the final round on TV and enjoy the Masters sandwiches.

When he first started doing it, Katcher befriended a couple that owned Jay's Music, which was located right outside the gates of Augusta National.

"I'd park at Jay's and I have a refrigerated cooler. I plug in my cooler, fill it up with ice to get it cool. On Saturday, I go into old pro shop and buy a few token items, and then I would ask the people there for extra bags. Now, with my extra bags I go next door...where they sell the sandwiches and I would count out—10, 12, 14 egg salad, 16 pimento cheese, 10 chicken cutlets, ham and cheese, Masters clubs—and I would start filling up these bags, carefully stacking the sandwiches in a way they couldn't get crushed.

"I get up to 100 or 120 sandwiches, which are incredibly heavy. And the physics of the sandwiches change, because they start pushing on each other. I've done it so many years in a row that the women at the register recognize me and they're like, 'New York, right?' I mean, who comes in and buys 100 sandwiches? I also get chocolate chip cookies, the white chocolate, and some of the caramel clusters.

"The bags are heavy. I like to get both bags about equal weight, because I like to be balanced. And I would walk all the way back to the store (Jay's) —a 12- to 14-minute walk. I have this enormous electric cooler and I pack it with the sandwiches and drive up to Virginia to the Omni Hotel, which is about halfway home. I then have to take the cooler out of the car, put it on a dolly to get it to the hotel room and plug it into the wall in the room.

"I don't drive all the way back, because it's 800 miles to New York. I stay at the hotel, sleep over, and drive back to New York

in the morning. I would get home about 1:00 PM, just in time
for the live TV broadcast to start."

The trick for Katcher is when he leaves Augusta, which is
difficult depending on what's going on in the tournament and
who he wants to watch.

"I always leave Augusta later that I want to," he said. "It
depends on the weather, and it depends on the things that go on.
I'd always be sitting at 18th green and Tiger would be finishing
late and I'd be with all my friends and I don't want to leave. It's
like five-and-a-half hours to Virginia."

The end game?

"I go back to my apartment and I invite a limited group
over," Katcher said. "Most people don't deserve sandwiches like
that. So I have a very small circle of people who come over and
watch the Masters and eat really fresh Masters sandwiches. So,
when you're having the egg salad sandwiches and pimento cheese
while you're watching the round live, it's exotic. No one else in
the world is doing that. Certainly no one in New York. I always
thought it would be sort of a nice touch.

"It was just a natural thing to do. I'm always looking for
something interesting to glean from any event I go to, and food
has always been an aspect of something I can control. If I can
buy it, I can bring it."

Katcher also will share the sandwiches with select people from
his workplace.

"When I was in the office in the earlier days, a bigger circle
of people would know that I'm well-known for going to the
Masters and that I would bring sandwiches back," he said. "It's
like a currency. I come in on Monday and, to the people who
I like, I would bring in the egg salad, chicken sandwiches, ham
and cheese, pimento cheese—and people would be like, 'Wow.'

"It was just an exotic thing to share with people. And it was very unique, and I always look at it like the movie *Smoky and the Bear*—like I was driving moonshine from the South to the North, hauling those sandwiches up, a very special cargo. I've never lost a batch, never had a power outage."

Katcher is proud of his sandwich scheme, saying, "You can't get them anywhere in the world except at the Masters. It's a very particular thing."

"I consider myself an unofficial ambassador for the Masters," Katcher said. "I'm a big supporter of the club and the membership and the tournament, and I think by spreading those sandwiches it sort of makes people more aware of it. There's a magic with the Masters and their sandwiches."

———

The Journey

Katcher used to start his Masters week by leaving New York City at 5:00 AM Sunday to arrive to Augusta by about at 5:00 PM.

"But 12 hours in the car hurts," he said. "The whole week is so physically taxing that I figured out a way to go Saturday, drive halfway, get up Sunday morning, and drive the other half to Augusta. I arrive Sunday 3:00 or 4:00 PM. I think I know more people in Augusta than I know in New York at this point. I've met a lot of people and made a lot of good friends I see each year that I go."

Katcher begins his Masters week by attending the Monday morning practice round and he brings two big Canon cameras, because—unlike during the tournament rounds—photography for fans is permitted during the practice rounds. He does the same thing on Tuesday and Wednesday.

"On Monday, Tuesday, and Wednesday mornings, if it's good weather, I'm on the course at 10:00 in the morning and I go to photograph certain things that are interesting to me. Generally, it's not the players, but landscapes and different elements of the tournament and the course that I like to take pictures of.

"One reason for going the entire week is weather," Katcher went on. "Suppose you go for one day and it's a crazy storm, which they seem to get every year, and your day aligns with that day, you're done. If you go for a whole week, it allows you to endure one or two of those days but still have at least one of those blue-bird, beautiful days."

———

His First Time

Katcher snuck into Augusta National at his first Masters.

"It was 2000, before 9/11, there were no scanners, no metal detectors," he recalled. "I had $2,000 in my pocket and I was trying to buy a ticket. I had no idea what I was doing. It was my first time there. I would have $2,000, trying to buy a ticket and addressing people who were streaming into the Masters. They wouldn't even look at me. It was as if I didn't exist. The money didn't make a difference.

"At the end of that day, I was sunburned and tired and it was 5:00 PM. Now I'm watching the security guards and their rhythm and I timed my walk and as the security guard looked away, I walked right in. That was the first time I ever saw the grass and everything. It was pretty special.

"The next year, I met a guy who walked me in for $500. He would have two badges, he would give me one, we would walk in together and as soon as we got deeper into the course, he would take the badge back and go do it again. And then I was sort of like exposed. I'd go sit up in the stands."

That, however, wasn't easy for Katcher, whose paranoia about getting caught threatened to get the best of him.

"I had one of the great panic attacks of all time," he recalled. "The first time the guy was going to walk me in, I got about 10 feet from them swiping the badge and I had a God-awful anxiety attack and froze. This guy had to sit on a bench with me for 15 minutes while I calmed down and steeled myself for the walk-through. He sat with me on the bench and talked me off the ledge.

"He was a ticket broker who turned into someone I dealt with for several years. Then I ended up with a more local guy for a few years. Now, I have friends who have an extra badge that they give me every year."

Katcher's initial impetus to go to the Masters was Tiger Woods.

"I realized in 2000 that watching him hit golf shots was super historic, and I was going to commit to getting my eyes on that in person, feeling it and watching it and understanding what it was for him to play there," Katcher said. "So that first time I went, I committed to as long as he's still playing, I would still go to the Masters. I've been more times than he has now. When I'd go and he's not there I'd sort of walk around aimlessly, because I'm not tied to his tee off times and following him."

———

Ritual

For Katcher, the real fun begins on Thursday, for the opening round. That's when the competition begins—not just for the players in the Masters field, but for Katcher and his obsession with getting to the 18th green before anyone else to place his folding Masters chair in the first row along the ropes, pin high to the left of the green.

"I get to the gate at 5:00 in the morning Thursday," Katcher said. "The gates open at 8:00. That's when you need to get there to be on the front of the line. There's an interesting clique of people that I've gotten to know over the years that do the same thing as I do.

"I started doing this by myself early on, and naturally wanted to be there early to get to 18 to put my seat there. And by doing it so many times, I've met a group of people who've come from all over...about 12 of us, from Tampa, Minnesota, the Carolinas. We're like a family now. We see each other only that week. We watch each other's backs, save each other's place in line, take care of each other on the course. It's a very intimate family-level relationship.

"We only see each other on those mornings once a year. Everyone has their own story. I have developed a position of seniority doing that, and there's only a handful of people who walk faster than I do, because you can't run. [Ed. note: Running is prohibited on the Augusta National grounds.] I've developed relationships with the guards and the members who are on the committee who oversee that entrance I go in from.

"There are different gates. I go in Gate 9. From Gate 9, you can get to hole Nos. 1, 18, 7, 4, and others. Everyone has their own schtick about what's valuable to them, and they go to that. There are the '18ers,' the '1ers,' and everyone has their own idea. Mine is 18. The folks that want to be at No. 16 go to Gate 2 and enter there."

Katcher said the weather is always a challenge, particularly with how early he arrives to the gates.

"The weather forces you to bring all kinds of different clothes," Katcher said. "I wear long underwear on some mornings, because it can be 30 degrees and you've got to sit there for three hours—two hours until the sun comes up. So, it can be a pretty brutal thing. And then you're on the course until the sun goes down, so these are three long days for me. Brutal, after three practice rounds and three rounds of golf, 16-hour days.

"The amount of work—getting up at 4:30, getting there at 5:00, waiting it out, and being released to enter the grounds and racing up the hill...you're always nervous you're not going to get the spot you want. You know the butterflies a professional athlete has before competition? No matter how good you are, there are some stages where they have butterflies. That's us. We're pros at what we do, but our hearts start racing when those gates open. It's very stressful.

"Once you get to 18 and put your chair down, you can breathe for the first time. I am a professional at that. Once we get the chairs down, my buddy will go get coffee and I will watch the chairs, guard the chairs and make sure nothing is moved."

The chair culture at Augusta National for the Masters is unique. When patrons—that's the required name for what the rest of us call "fans" or "spectators"—place their chairs down, the unspoken Masters etiquette is that no one can move them. It's like kids saving a place in line at school and that place actually is saved.

The chairs are purchased at Augusta National. Patrons cannot bring their own chair onto the grounds. So there are thousands of those green folding chairs with a Masters logo all over the golf course, ringing greens, and tee boxes.

"The etiquette is if the person isn't there, you're allowed to sit in the chair," Katcher said. "If the person who owns the chair comes, you simply get out of the chair. If you're smart, you have your name on the back of your chair so you can always find it. I put my chair, if I can, right on a metal post on the ropes on the 18th green, because when errant approach shots fly in and the chairs have to be moved, I always know my chair is going back to the same place."

Bizarre as some of the quirks of the culture are, Katcher is not put off by them. To the contrary, he wholeheartedly embraces them.

"The whole history there and all of their traditions attracted me to the Masters," Katcher said. "I was attracted right off the bat. I respected it right away, I enjoyed it and wanted to be a part of it more and more. It's why I go back. If you're willing to put in the effort, what you get back out of that—front row, pin high on 18 at Augusta, is pretty damned special. And I can control that."

Saturday is the most challenging day for Katcher, because the club allows members onto the grounds earlier than the general public on Saturdays and, Katcher said, "they can take up the entire front row, sometimes all of it, with their chairs."

Katcher insists that—regardless of the drama that might unfold in the final round—he never regrets not staying in Augusta on Sundays.

"Early on, I used to stay on Sundays and psychologically it's not the right thing for me, because it's so anticlimactic," Katcher said. "You're there the whole week, you're there Sunday—and you can't get in the front row on Sunday, because the members ring the first two rows on Sunday. Somebody wins and then, what do I have left in front of me? I've got 800 miles of driving to do, and that 800 miles is torture driving home.

"So, I've learned to go back on Saturday with something to look forward to when I get home on Sunday," he continued. "I'm so worn out from the week that I collapse by the time I get home.

I get to watch the entire Sunday round sitting in air conditioning on a couch watching a high-definition TV picture. And when it's over, I get to turn it off and go to sleep instead of having to drive 800 miles home. Three practice rounds, three tournament rounds are perfect. Sundays are just not for me."

A couple of Katcher's most thrilling Masters moments had nothing to do with the actual golf on the course.

"In 2004, I'm sitting on 18, second row on the Saturday and I helped a member with some of his chairs after play was finished," he recalled. "His friends had left and there were about seven chairs there. I asked him if he needed some help and I helped him we fold up the chairs.

"It turns out, he and his family were staying in the Eisenhower Cabin and he invited me in. He took me upstairs. It was magical. I had to take off my shoes, walk by State Troopers strapped with weapons at the entrance. We spent some time in there. There are hand-painted oil paintings by Mr. Eisenhower that hang on the walls. Just to see that was very special."

He also used to have some unique moments in the old gravel parking lot adjacent to the main entrance before the new practice facility was built where the parking lot used to be.

"I always carry my golf clubs in the trunk of my car, and I used to hit balls off the gravel driveway," Katcher said. "That was as close as I've come to playing Augusta."

A couple of years ago, he also got an invite to Berckman's Place, the newest state-of-the-art corporate gluttonous experience of excess that is located on the other side of the fifth hole and offers replica putting greens, gads of food and beverages, and a unique souvenir shop that sells items that aren't available in the main merchandise shops.

"Those tickets go for $5,000 a day; I got in for $1,200, had the food, putted, the special pro shop, did the whole thing,"

Katcher said. "But it's almost too good. You're sitting 50 yards away from people playing golf and you're watching them on these TVs. It's too close, it's too nice."

As for accommodations in Augusta, Katcher has upgraded to better and better accommodations over the years.

"I started at the Masters Inn, where the carpets were wet and you wouldn't walk barefoot," he said. "As I got a little more advanced, I graduated to some townhouses down on Berckmans Road [near the club]. I rented one or two other houses, rented a house at Palmetto Golf Club from a family that I've become close to. The past seven years, I've rented the same house less than a mile from the course."

Katcher estimates that he spends about $10,000 on average for each trip.

Is he ever asked by friends or family if he's nuts for spending that kind of money, getting up so early in the morning, and following his fastidious routines so rigidly?

"It's a well-respected, religious pilgrimage for me," Katcher said. "People know I'm known for it. They respect it. They tell me, 'Wow, keep doing it.'"

What's left now for Katcher, who's done about everything you can do as a fan at the Masters, is to elevate his experience.

"I aspire to go in there, inside the ropes, and eat lunch outside the clubhouse where the members and players eat," he said. "So I'm working on getting a badge to get in there. That's my next evolution. I'm sick and tired of getting up at 4:00 in the morning. So I'm working on a pass where someone can give me a Trophy Club and I can get there at 7:30 and walk in with the members. I can put my chair down without having a heart attack.

"I always thought that someone would ask me to join the club," Katcher said. "I thought in some fantastical way that, because of my devotion and how much I respect and support the club, someone would recognize that and think of me as a good member who would add values to the committees. I'm just a big fan of the way they run things and how special and thoughtful they are doing that. It's the way I think, and I would love to participate in it. I don't deserve it, but it would be special."

Chapter 13

HONORARY STARTERS

"Ladies and gentlemen. The [present year] Masters Tournament is officially underway."

These are the words delivered by the Augusta National chairman to the smattering of fans who gather at the first tee early on the Thursday morning of every Masters to witness the traditional honorary starters ceremony.

To borrow an oft-used line from the great CBS Sports golf announcer Jim Nantz, it is "a tradition like no other."

They've been trotting out some of the Masters legends from yesteryear to strike ceremonial tee shots off the first tee since 1963, when Jock Hutchison and Fred McLeod did the honors. Hutchison won the 1920 PGA Championship and the 1921 British Open, becoming the first American to win the Claret Jug. McLeod, a Scot, won the 1908 U.S. Open.

The reason those two players were chosen for the honor?

Both had won the Senior PGA Championship, which began at Augusta National. Hutchison won the inaugural edition in 1937 and McLeod won in its second year in 1938. They actually began the tradition informally in 1954 with both players not only hitting the ceremonial opening tee shots, but playing the first nine or all 18 holes before withdrawing from the tournament.

Hutchison continued in the role until 1973. McLeod went on until 1976.

From 1977 to 1980, the Masters didn't have honorary starters. But the tradition was revived in 1981 with Byron Nelson and Gene Sarazen.

Sarazen was well known for famously making an albatross in the final round—"the shot heard 'round the world"—on his way to winning the 1935 Masters. Nelson won green jackets in 1937 and 1942.

In 1984, Sam Snead joined Sarazen and Nelson and the three of them continued through 1999, when Sarazen was an honorary starter for the final time before dying four months later.

Nelson stopped as an honorary starter in 2001, five years before dying in 2006, and Snead stopped in 2002, dying the following month at the age of 89.

From 2003 to 2006, there were no honorary starters. The tradition was again revived in 2007 when Arnold Palmer did it solo until 2010, when Jack Nicklaus joined Palmer. Gary Player joined Palmer and Nicklaus in 2012 to complete the "Big Three" as the trio of Masters honorary starters.

As of 2019, Nicklaus and Player remained as the two honorary starters.

For a tournament that stands so proudly on tradition and ceremony, this is one of the coolest of them all. And for the fans who gather around the first tee box and line the ropes down both sides of the fairway, it's well worth the early wakeup call to witness it.

"I always wanted to go see them tee off and experience that," Phil Mickelson said. "I went there in 2010 and I ended up winning the tournament that year. But I got up early and went to watch them tee off and it was a pretty cool moment. What those guys have done for the game of golf is amazing, and to be able to be there and see them start the tournament was pretty cool."

Paul Azinger recalled playing in his first Masters in 1987 and making it his business to get out to the first tee to see the honorary starters ceremony.

"I booked it out there to watch Gene Sarazen and Byron Nelson and Sam Snead hit the first tee shot; I was never going to miss that," Azinger said. "I couldn't believe I wasn't by myself out there, it was so early. I did it a lot. I stopped going once Sarazen and Nelson stopped. It's crazy when you get old and look back at all that and reminisce about it."

No honorary starter ceremony has ever been as powerful and poignant as the morning of April 6, 2017.

That was the first Masters in 61 years that began without Palmer present.

"The King" had died the previous fall at age 87 and the honorary starters ceremony went on without him. In the literal sense, anyway. Though he was not there physically, Palmer was there in spirit. Everyone in attendance could feel it.

During the 2016 ceremony, Palmer, not strong enough to take a swing anymore, sat in a white lawn chair and watched Nicklaus and Player hit their drives. Five months later, he died.

On the Thursday morning of April 6, 2017, that white lawn chair was again on the tee box, with the green jacket from one of Palmer's four Masters wins draped over it. Nicklaus, 77 at the time, wiped tears from his eyes, tipped his cap, and looked to the sky before hitting his drive into the fairway. Player, 81 at the time, also rubbed tears from his eyes and somehow hit his drive into the fairway as well.

Before balls were struck, Billy Payne, then the Augusta National chairman, asked for a moment of silence so everyone could "give their own personal goodbye to the wonderful man." He then made a few remarks.

"Good morning and welcome to the 2017 Masters," Payne began, flanked by Palmer's wife, Kit. "It is a wonderful, but in one respect, a difficult day. For the first time in many, many decades someone is obviously missing from the first tee. The almost unbearable sadness that we all feel by the passing of Arnold Palmer is only surpassed by the love and affection for him.

"Arnold Palmer was more than The King, a title he justifiably deserved by virtue of his four Masters victories and more than 70 PGA Tour and Senior Tour wins," Payne went on. "Arnold Palmer was my friend. He was your friend. Despite all his fame and fortune, he always had time for all of us. A smile, an autograph, a photo—he was always giving. But it still hurts so bad that he is not here with us today."

Payne recalled all the years of worship for Palmer at Augusta, particularly on that traditional ceremonial first tee shot.

"As he would walk to this very tee for this ceremony we would point and shout above the cheers to our kids and grandkids," Payne said. "'Look, look, it's Arnold Palmer!' And the kids would radiate smiles because they knew they were seeing a legend. And you know what? He would always smile back. That's the Arnold Palmer we remember, we miss, and we'll forever love."

Palmer played his last competitive round at the Masters in 1983 and had been part of the ceremonial first tee shot group for years—until 2015, when he struck his final ceremonial first tee shot.

"We knew this day would come," Payne said. "We counted our blessings over the last several years as his health was beginning to decline but his smile and his graciousness never changed."

Everyone in attendance was given white buttons with green lettering that read, I AM A MEMBER OF ARNIE'S ARMY.

There was an immense and heavy sadness that hung in the cool spring Georgia air that Thursday morning. But it was a celebration, too.

Player later called Payne's words "extremely eloquent, very touching."

Recalling Palmer being restricted to that white chair for the ceremony the year before, the last time most people had seen him in public, Player recalled, "When he sat on the chair last year and they called his name, you know, a lot of people don't stand up. But Arnold could hardly walk to the first tee and he stood up because he had been taught to stand up.

"He gave a little wave, and that was very touching to me, and I could see him doing it in that chair today."

Former LPGA star Nancy Lopez, who'd become a close friend of Palmer's and frequently attends the Masters, told the *Pittsburgh Post-Gazette*, "For him not to be well enough to hit the opening tee shot with Jack and Gary broke my heart. He's so proud, and I could see it was killing him to be sitting there watching. I went to hug him, and that was the first time he didn't stand up to give me a hug. So I kind of knew. He got choked up talking about his fans. And thinking of that makes me cry. The reason he always gave so much of himself to them was because he loved them."

The following year, 2017, was the first Masters Palmer had not attended since 1955. It was the first Masters in which he, Nicklaus, and Palmer, referred to as the "Big Three," were not together. Now the Big Three had been reduced to a Big Two.

"There will be other big threes, but I don't know if you'll ever have another big three that will live together like we did," Player said. "It was a very, very unusual time in history, and it will be interesting to see if there is again. And it was a privilege and we all appreciated each other, which was a great friendship. It's hard to be highly competitive against people and have a great friendship. And yet I sit here today and Jack Nicklaus is my best friend in the world."

Between the three of them, Palmer, Nicklaus, and Player combined to win 34 major championships. They were competitors but they were friends, too.

"I think that we had a very unusual friendship among competitors," Player said. "It was so fiercely competitive, and we made it very clear we wanted to beat the hell out of each other. When we did, we looked the other man in the eye and said: 'Well done.' So we built a friendship, traveling extensively around the world.

"We won something like 50 major championships—senior and regular tour—and we must have won over 350 golf tournaments. And to have longevity has been a special gift. To come here [that day] and to be on the tee with Arnold being a part of us, it was gratifying and sad, because everything shall pass. But it was nice to have him on the tee. I dedicated my first tee shot to him in respect."

Memories of Palmer dominated conversations that 2017 Masters week without him. At the annual Tuesday night Champions Dinner, Nicklaus and Player were asked to share memories of Palmer by everyone, and they obliged.

Of the seven career major championships Palmer won during his career, four of them were at Augusta National. Palmer and the Masters and Augusta National were synonymous.

"The popularity of the game was really stimulated by Arnold," Nicklaus said. "The Masters made Arnold in many ways because of his wins in '58, '60, '62, and '64, but the other way around, I think Arnold made the Masters. Arnold put the Masters on the map and with his rise and his popularity, the Masters rose the same. I think they were both very good for each other and very synonymous with each other."

The year before, Palmer's final appearance at Augusta in 2016, and his final visit to the first tee for the Thursday morning tradition, Palmer's health had been in decline and there were questions about whether he'd be able to hit a shot alongside Nicklaus and Player.

"I think that everybody was happy to see Arnold out on the tee," Nicklaus said at the time. "I think Arnold was happy to be on the tee. I think he would have preferred to hit a golf ball. I talked to him at the Masters Champions Dinner [two nights earlier] and I said, 'Arnold, when you're out there, what if we just take you up and had you hit, I don't care if you putt it off the tee, I think everybody would love to have you do anything.'

"He said, 'Let me think about it.' I said, 'Okay.' So [that Thursday] morning, I talked to him and I said, 'What do you want to do?' He said, 'I'm good.' I said, 'Fine, let's leave it alone.' So I think probably the right thing. Arnold's balance is not good and that's what they were worried about. But I think he was delighted to be out there. I think we were delighted to have him there. I think both Gary and I felt it was more about Arnold [that] morning than anything else and I think that was just fine."

Curtis Strange, the two-time U.S. Open winner who went to Wake Forest, where Palmer went to school, said the Masters "will never be the same" without The King.

"The tournament will go on and players will come and go, but there will be a void there," Strange said. "I grew up with Arnold Palmer in my household as everybody did. And then the first time I played the Masters was in '75. I went down there and saw really what Arnie's Army and Arnold Palmer and the people were all about. It was the first time I had ever seen him in his world. And it was spectacular.

"There was a connection there between Arnold and the people and the people and Arnold that was unlike anything I had ever seen in my life before and since. The way he reacted to them and them to him was something special. And even [in 2016], when he wasn't doing well, and just for him to make the effort to go and be a part of it, something he loved so dearly, it showed me that it really was a connection there over the years and that they truly loved each other."

Andy North, like Strange a two-time U.S. Open champion, adored Palmer like everyone else. And, like everyone who attended the Masters, whether as a player, spectator, or member of the media, he could not wait to see Palmer hit one of those ceremonial first tee shots every year, because it made him feel like he was a part of something special, something historic.

"I remember as a kid, really the first time you ever saw golf on TV, or at least I did, was Arnold," North said. "That changed the way we looked at our sport. The last year he played there, I'm one of those guys that used to go out on Thursday morning and love watching the guys hit those first tee shots. That was always special. And there's going to be a big empty spot at the Masters because Arnold's not there."

Jim Nantz, from CBS, recalled Palmer, in 2016 at his final Masters, agreeing to come to Butler Cabin to be interviewed after what would be his final appearance for that ceremonial first tee shot.

Nantz had asked Palmer about doing the interview weeks earlier and they agreed, because of Palmer's failing health, that they'd wait to decide until that Thursday morning to see if Palmer was up for the taping.

"I met him in the clubhouse after the shot and we're sitting around a table and he looked at me and said, 'What do you think?' I said, 'It's totally up to you,'" Nantz recalled. "And he looked at me and gave me that Arnie thumbs-up and said, 'Let's do it.' So we got the Butler Cabin ready to go and got Arnold to the cabin and we made it very clear if it was a struggle or the words wouldn't come out cleanly we'd stop and no one would ever see it.

"When the lights went on and the first question was about showing up here in 1955, it was like turning back the clock. You could see the look on his face. When the lights came on, Arnold was on."

Nantz, who has witnessed and called some of the most memorable moments that have ever occurred at Augusta National, said that moment was one he'll "never forget."

"He never returned," Nantz said. "That was his last visit to the Masters."

PART FIVE

FRIDAY

Chapter 14

ARNIE

F ew sporting events in the world produce moments like the
Masters does at Augusta National every April. These moments
have become a rite of springtime and they often spawn memories
of a lifetime for those fortunate enough to witness them in person
or even through a television screen.

On Friday afternoon, April 10, 2004, at about 2:15 PM, one
of those unforgettable moments unfolded simultaneously on holes
No. 6 and No. 16, where the two greens are half a sand wedge
apart, separated by only spectators, pine needles and a few tall
pine trees.

The hill situated below the sixth tee and overlooking the
16th green, where fans sprawl out on the grass as if they were
chilling out at Jones Beach on an 80-degree day watching the
waves roll in off the Atlantic, is one of the finest places in sports
to watch the action unfold.

While Jack Nicklaus was arriving at the 16th green, Arnold
Palmer, playing in his 50th consecutive—and final—Masters,
had just stuck his tee shot to within five feet of the flag on
the sixth green to the delight of the throng of fans packed into
the area.

Then, as Nicklaus was surveying his 30-foot birdie putt on the 16th green, Palmer and his larger-than-life image were silhouetted against the afternoon sun as he walked over the top of the hill and headed down toward the sixth green. Nicklaus, now watching Palmer, removed his cap and lifted it in the air in honor of The King and then gave him the thumbs up, a customary Palmer gesture.

Palmer, catching eyes with Nicklaus, returned the love, taking his cap off, giving the thumbs up and waving. The place was delirious.

Moments later, Nicklaus and Palmer were standing over their respective putts at the exact same moment, Nicklaus sinking his three-footer for par and Palmer barely missing his five-foot birdie attempt and tapping in for par.

With that being Palmer's final round of his final Masters, it was the last time a moment like that would ever play out, and it was one to be forever inscribed into the memory banks for all who were there to see it.

It was the best of all Masters moments on the Friday of the 68th edition of the storied event.

About three hours after that memorable moment, which would not be captured on television, because back then the front nine of the Masters was not televised, Palmer would amble his way up the steep, uphill 18th fairway to the green for the last time at a Masters at age 74.

Palmer, winner of four green jackets, all coming in a dizzying seven-year span, was playing in his 50th and final Masters, shooting a pair of 84s on his way to missing the cut.

"I'm not going to make a big, long speech today," Palmer said. "I'm through. I've had it. I'm done. Cooked. Washed up. Finished, whatever you want to say. It's time."

When asked what it felt like to walk up 18 for one final time at Augusta, Palmer said, "Use your imagination, and you will understand. I thought about how many times I walked up that 18th fairway. I can think of the four times I won the Masters. I can think of a couple of times that I didn't win that I felt like I should have won.

"I can think of the fans that have supported me. I listened to them, and of course most of them have something to say when I'm walking up that fairway. Emotion? A lot. Sometimes I just get tired and emotion overrules and runs away with me. I'm not upset about that. The fact is that one of the things I want to do was what I did today, and that was to finish 50 years at Augusta. All my family is here, and that has never happened before at any golf tournament. That's very special. It's something I wanted. I just wanted them to see what happens."

Palmer went on to say, "Augusta and this golf tournament has been about [as much] a part of my life as anything other than my family. I don't think I could ever separate myself from this club and this tournament. I may not be present, I may not be here, but I'll still be a part of what happens here, only because I want to be."

Palmer was a presence at the Masters for 62 years—50 as a player, 10 as an honorary starter, and two more years for the time in between when he wasn't sure he wanted to hit the ceremonial first tee shot as an honorary starter.

Palmer died at age 87 in September of 2016, so the 2017 Masters was the first since 1954 Palmer was not in attendance, and it was an emotional week because of it. The highlight of the week was a powerful ceremony at the first tee led by then-chairman Billy Payne, who had an empty chair set up in honor of The King with his green jacket draped over the back of it.

"It will never be the same," said Curtis Strange, who had a special bond with Palmer because of their Wake Forest connection. (Strange went to Wake Forest on an Arnold Palmer Scholarship established by The King at his alma mater.)

Palmer was the first player to win the Masters four times. Jack Nicklaus would eventually break his record with six and Tiger Woods tied him in 2019 when he won his fourth. But Palmer could have had more.

In 1959, as the defending champion, he was tied for the lead after three rounds. But Palmer made a triple-bogey at the par-3 12th and finished third that year, two shots behind winner Art Wall Jr., who started the day six shots behind Palmer.

In 1961, Palmer was vying to become the tournament's first repeat winner, needed only a par at the 72nd to give him a one-shot victory over Gary Player. But Palmer hit his approach shot from the fairway into a greenside bunker and then bladed his next shot across the green and took a double bogey to lose by one shot to Player.

It was Palmer's play around holes No. 11, 12, and 13 on the far corner of Augusta National in 1958 en route to his first Masters win that inspired *Sports Illustrated* writer Herbert Warren Wind to use the expression "Amen Corner" to describe those three iconic holes.

"Arnie's Army," the nickname used to describe the horde of spectators following Palmer as if he were a pied piper, was born in Augusta because of the soldiers at nearby Fort Gordon who manned the leaderboards at the Masters and openly rooted for Palmer.

The late Frank Chirkinian, the pioneering TV producer who ran the Masters telecasts on CBS for 40 years, once described how

Palmer had become a magnet to the camera during his back-nine charge in 1960, saying, "I thought, 'Holy mackerel, who is this guy?' He absolutely fired up the screen. It was quite obvious this was the star. It was electrifying."

Chapter 15

DALY

It is late afternoon on the eve of the Masters, a little after 6:00 PM on Wednesday. The annual Par-3 Contest is long finished. The players' practice rounds have been completed.

And yet, there is a line of fans snaking through a parking lot waiting to purchase merchandise. The people are not lined up to buy Masters souvenirs, though. They are not even on Augusta National property.

They are in a Hooters parking lot, located about three or four John Daly tee shots down Washington Road from Magnolia Lane, patiently waiting to meet Daly, shake his hand, express their love for him, and score items from the John Daly brand.

There are boxes of "Grip it and Rip it" T-shirts, logoed ball markers, head covers, license plates, hats, CDs, pin flags, towels, beverage coozies, belts, and Loudmouth apparel, including shorts and skorts. There, too, are cans of Daly's branded "Grip it and Sip it" beverages made with iced tea and vodka or sweet tea, lemonade, and vodka.

Most importantly, the people are there to meet Daly, have him sign autographs, express their adulation for him, and take selfies with them.

Daly has been posted up with his RV and a bunch of tables with his merchandise outside the gates of Augusta National during Masters week since 1997, hawking souvenirs.

With a cigarette hanging limply from his lips, he engages with all who stop by. And, if you buy it, he'll sign it. He'll actually sign anything you ask him to—whether you've made a purchase or not.

"I've probably signed about 20 sets of boobs this week and about 30 asses," Daly said as he signed for fans in line rapid-fire before the 2018 Masters. "And they are fine asses, too. I'll sign any ass, it doesn't matter. Like Jesus, I love 'em all."

It is an unmistakable sideshow bordering on a carnival act—as it always has been since Daly first started doing this.

"I just figured it's a good way to sell the brand," Daly said while signing the package of someone's pimento cheese sandwich from the Masters. "When I started back in '97 with the logo, I just figured it was a great way to sell it. We've got a great relationship with Hooters. I help them and they help me this week. It's a good week. The money doesn't really matter to me. It's just so much fun to be out here, seeing people, getting the brand out."

It used to be a sad look when he first started doing this: Daly, with his incredible golf skills being wasted, peddling cheesy T-shirts and hats from a parking lot outside of Augusta National instead of bombing long drives down the fairways of Augusta National and competing for a green jacket.

Daly played in 12 Masters in his career and had one top-10 finish—a tie for third in 1993, his second try. He missed the cut in four of his final five Masters, including the last three, his final invite coming in 2006.

He's in his fifties now and is a part-time player on the Champions Tour, complaining of arthritis in his knees that prevents him from walking more than six or seven holes. So, this road show is pretty much his full-time gig. The Masters stop is the 11th in a 37-week tour that Daly has scheduled this year.

What once looked and felt like a sad small-town carnival act has become a wildly popular and profitable venture for Daly, who sets up shop at about 8:00 AM and is still selling and signing well past dinnertime.

You never know who's going to stop by and see Daly. Daly said Eric Trump was over the other day. Former Cowboys great defensive lineman Ed "Too Tall" Jones has visited, as has Cowboys head coach Jason Garrett.

Dave Saracino, a high-ranking executive with BIC (pens and lighters), befriended Daly years ago and visits him regularly.

"This says that he's us," Saracino said, looking around at the mob scene jockeying for position to get close to Daly. "There's nothing else you can say except he's the real deal. He's as great as he ever was. If he could putt, he'd win everything."

Hearing that backhanded compliment, Daly interjected, saying, "I can't putt? It ain't my putting, man. It's my attitude."

If you ask the masses who line up all day to see Daly as a folk hero, they have no problem with his attitude.

Cory Moore, a private security guard who travels with Daly in his RV, said, "I have a video of about 200 people chanting his name the night before last when he walked off the bus."

Moore stays around Daly's RV until about 3:30 in the morning every day to make sure people don't bother him late at night.

"I've found people knocking on the bus," Moore said. "They're just having fun. They're excited to see him, because nobody else comes and does this."

The only trouble that Daly has encountered with his Hooters setup came in 2018, when his RV was hit by a car. Daly said the RV was hit when a driver tried to make a U-turn but lost control of the car. He said he tweaked his knee while trying to get out of harm's way.

"It whaled into the front of the bus," his fiancée, Anna Cladakis, told GolfChannel.com. "John dove out of the way."

It's difficult to properly measure who loves who more: Daly or his fans.

"The greatest thing for me is when someone comes up and says, 'My son started playing golf because of you,' or, 'I started playing golf because of you,'" Daly said. "We're like family. It's the Hooters tradition. It's just awesome. We've got like 20,000 to 30,000 people coming through here."

Daly hopes to be at Hooters for as long as he can stand, an institution outside of the real institution in town. Augusta National, however, has been purchasing swaths of land along Washington Road with rumors of building another golf course and expanding its brand.

That land expansion project has been creeping its way down Washington Road toward Hooters, with rumors that the club eventually wants its own exit ramp off of Interstate 20 to expedite its patrons' arrival to the Masters.

That, of course, would be a crushing blow to the endless rows of businesses along Washington Road, which depend on that Masters traffic stopping at their stores. Hooters is one of those. Daly, however, doesn't believe the expansion is going to take over Hooters.

"From what I understand, I was told they did a 20-year lease and they put me in the lease," Daly said. "I doubt I'll be here by then—I'll be 73—but you never know. As long as they don't get mad at me for signing girls' asses, I'm okay."

The green jackets of Augusta National, as they do for a number of other places, have seemingly ignored Daly's sideshow...or at least looked the other way. Whether or not the club embraces it is an entirely different story.

"Hey, I've always had respect for the members and the guys in there," Daly said of Augusta National. "It's really been the only place where I haven't been in trouble."

Paul Azinger, who, like Daly, has sometimes been a bit irreverent compared to the general conservative golf establishment, said he didn't know "what to think" about the Daly show outside Augusta National when he first saw it.

"It just felt like John Daly being John Daly, renegade, building a brand," Azinger said. "He was a brand all unto his own because of his wild nature, that image with the mullet. It became pretty clear pretty quickly that he had a drinking problem and gambling problem and he was able to admit those. He's one of those obsessive compulsives. You have to be that way to play great golf, and he epitomized that.

"The one great thing Daly always had going for him was he didn't really have any secrets, which is a pretty nice way to live your life. Not having any secrets and being an open book to all who loved him, it made them love him more. He hit it a mile. He had all the ingredients to be super popular."

Azinger, though, still to this day wonders aloud how Daly didn't have more success inside the gates and ropes at Augusta.

"I thought Augusta was perfect for John Daly, as high as he hit it, as far as he hit it, and the way he putted," Azinger said. "He had a magnificent short game. But I don't even remember him contending there. I think he was having performance anxiety. There was a lot going on inside his head."

Chapter 16

LEFTY

P hil Mickelson had won 21 tournaments on the PGA Tour by the time he arrived at Augusta National in April of 2004 to play in his 11th career Masters as a pro.

As had become a personal tradition for Mickelson, he would collect the flag from the 18th green pin after every one of those wins and present it to his grandfather, Al Santos, as a keepsake.

Around Christmas of 2003, Al Santos told his grandson, half-joking but serious, too, "I don't want any more of these Tour wins; I want a major."

For all of his previous successes—far from a career to sneeze at—Mickelson had played in 46 major championships as a professional without winning one. And it was becoming a *thing* for Mickelson, whose failure to capture a major despite his enormous talent essentially spawned the label: "Best player never to win a major."

Mickelson—and his grandfather, too—was tired of hearing his name associated with that label.

So, he went and won that 2004 Masters, breaking his 0-for-46 streak in majors. Unfortunately, his grandfather wasn't around to witness it or receive the flag from the 18th hole of Augusta

National. He died at the age of 97 in January 2004, shortly after he spoke those motivational words to his grandson.

"He said to me around that Christmas before he passed, 'This is your year,'" Mickelson recalled right after he won. "As that winning putt caught the left lip and fell in, I couldn't help but think he may have had something to do with it."

There a number of poignant, if spiritual, moments Mickelson remembered from that '04 Masters.

Moments before he left the house he had been renting to go play the most important round of golf of his life that Sunday morning of the final round, he looked at his wife, Amy, and said, "It feels different. It is different."

Heartbreak had become such a fabric of the Mickelson narrative in major championships. There was, for example, Payne Stewart seizing the moment from Mickelson at the 1999 U.S. Open at Pinehurst and David Toms doing the same thing at the 2001 PGA Championship. Both made putts on the final hole to beat Mickelson.

In that fateful final round in '04, it was Mickelson who seized every moment and exorcised every demon, carding birdies on five of the final seven holes to capture what would be the first of three green jackets he would win. He finished 9-under par overall and turned that final round into the most exhilarating final round since Jack Nicklaus won in 1986 at age 46.

Mickelson shot 31 on the back nine, the lowest total since Nicklaus shot 30 in 1986, and won it with an 18-foot downhill birdie putt on the 72nd hole.

He leaped into the air, with both arms and his putter raised to the sky, hugged caddie Jim "Bones" Mackay, and told him, "I did it!"

Finally, Mickelson was a major winner, a green jacket owner. The daredevil way Mickelson did it added to the thrill of victory.

He outdueled Ernie Els in a dazzling back nine that climaxed with a birdie on the 72nd and final hole to clinch the victory, only the fourth time in Masters history that had happened.

The exclamation point he put on the day was all Mickelson all the way in that it was an utter thrill ride to the end. The winning putt caught the left edge of the cup and spun tantalizingly around it before disappearing into the hole.

Mickelson marched immediately to his wife, Amy, lifted her in the air, and hugged her, and then he picked up his three-year-old daughter, Amanda, and said to her, "Daddy won. Can you believe it?"

Mickelson himself couldn't.

"This doesn't feel real," he said. "I can't believe this is happening."

He called it "an amazing day" and "a fulfillment of dreams," and said it was a moment "I'm going to relive in my mind forever and ever."

There were so many moments from which to choose for Mickelson on that magical day, beginning with the events leading up to that winning putt, with his playing partner and friend, Chris DiMarco, leaving his bunker shot two inches outside Mickelson's ball marker on the same line.

That DiMarco was going to have to give Mickelson a read on his eventual winning putt was one of those signs of fate that the fabled place simply offers up at the most poignant moments.

"Surreal," Mickelson called it.

"It was meant to be for him," DiMarco said afterward. "To be quite honest, I didn't think there was any way he would miss that putt. It was just time."

Mickelson said of the putt on 18, "The first thing went through my mind was my ball was on the same line that DiMarco missed from the same spot, and I thought I had missed it low.

But my ball rung around the cup and went in. And the first thing that went in my head was my grandfather nudged that ball in.

"We had that conversation before he passed away earlier that year, and he said to me, 'You're going to win the Masters this year.' So, in my head that was always what gave me that belief that this was my year. So, when that putt went in that conversation was the first thing that went on in my head."

Mickelson has never been short on confidence or the power of positive thinking. Every morning he wakes up optimistic about what's going to occur that day. He was on record long before 2004 in saying that he was going to win the Masters and he wasn't going to win just one major championship, he was going to win multiple majors.

He would go on to win the 2006 Masters and again in 2010. Those three Masters victories, coupled with the 2005 PGA Championship and 2013 British Open, give him five career majors, a mere U.S. Open victory short of an elusive and rare career Grand Slam, which only six players have accomplished.

"In '04, I had played so well at the start of the year and I had put in this extra time that I hadn't done in the past and I felt really prepared for that Masters," Mickelson said. "But you never know how it's going to play out. That front nine on Sunday just didn't go as I had planned."

He fixed that with the 31 on the back nine, which would vanquish a very good run by Ernie Els.

"It was when the putt went in on 12 that sparked the round," Mickelson said. "Ernie was ahead of me and he had already birdied 13. That putt on 12 was the big thing, because if I make that I'm really only one back and if that one doesn't go in then I've got a lot of ground to make up.

"When that putt on 12 went in, I knew I was going to birdie 13, because that hole sets up well for me. I hit a good drive and hit 7-iron so now I make birdie and I'm only one back with five holes to go. I didn't know where I was going to make up the ground but I felt I would."

When Mickelson failed to birdie the par-5 15th hole, it could have derailed his run.

"Not birdieing 15 was difficult, but I was playing so well it didn't bother me the way it normally would," he said. "Normally, I feel like I've got to birdie the par-5s, but I felt like I was playing so well that I would have chances the next three holes, which I ended up having.

"It was probably the most exciting moment in my career, to birdie the last hole to win by one. To win my first major, at the Masters, my favorite event, it was by far the most exciting moment of my career. The most fulfilling was winning the [2013] British Open, because I always knew I would win the Masters and I knew I would win it more than once. But the British Open? I didn't know if I would ever win that. So that first Masters was, by far, the greatest moment."

————

Witness to Final-Round Frenzy

Masters Sundays are, quite simply, as electric as they are unique to anything you'll ever experience if you're fortunate enough to witness one in person.

You don't need a TV or radio to keep you informed about what's going on around you. You can, instead, read the action based on the decibel level of the roars from particular holes and figure out exactly what's transpiring around the storied grounds. That 2004 Mickelson final round was the blueprint.

For example, as I walked toward Amen Corner to position myself to see the leaders come through the most fabled three holes in golf, a roar that more resembled a cheer for a game-winning touchdown in a football game emanated from the 11th hole.

As I waited to cross the 15th tee box, where Fred Couples was standing over his tee shot, the roars were so loud and sustained that Couples had to back off his shot three times. If you'd been to Augusta before, you knew this was not a birdie roar. It was an eagle roar—this one for a 220-yard K.J. Choi hole-out on the par-4 11th.

Once I arrived to Amen Corner and situated myself on a media grandstand that used to overlook the 11th, 12th, and 13th holes, I watched as Mickelson, one shot behind Els at the moment, stood over his birdie putt as the galleries at the 13th hole unleashed a roar so thunderous it could have been a game-winning Derek Jeter home run at Yankee Stadium.

It meant eagle for Els and a three-shot deficit for Mickelson, and Mickelson knew it. Still, he never backed off his putt and drained the must-make birdie to stay within two.

Once Mickelson putted out, I raced over to a grandstand on 15 that also overlooks the par-3 16th hole.

Just as I arrived there, Padraig Harrington delivered a hole-in-one on 16, leaving the massive crowds around that corner of the course delirious. Less than 10 minutes later, Kirk Triplett duplicated Harrington's feat and holed out on 16, falling to his back and lying on the tee box ground as the crowds erupted in disbelief.

At age 43 at the time and having played golf for some 20 years and watched it longer, I'd never seen a hole-in-one live. Suddenly, I'd seen two in less than 10 minutes.

A short time later, Els would march through and birdie No. 15 to get to 8-under-par while Mickelson was carding birdie on No. 13 to get to 6-under and the place was abuzz.

With Els approaching the 18th tee, Mickelson would then drain a 15-foot birdie putt on 16 to tie it at 8-under and the booming roar from there had those around the entire course in a state of bedlam, with fans racing to the 18th green to get a glimpse of the climax.

Els, who heard the sounds coming from 16 and knew exactly what it meant, called the noise "probably the loudest I've ever heard it."

It was never greater than when Mickelson, playing in the final group of the day and needing birdie to win, was on 18, where he delivered one of those signature Masters moments—the one that had eluded him through 10-plus frustrating near-miss years of no wins in majors—and it seemed you could hear the sounds from the crowd around 18, reverberating through the tall Georgia pines and all the way to Yankee Stadium in New York.

Shot of a Lifetime

Of the three Masters Mickelson has won, because of the way he executed his third victory at Augusta, none represented who he is more than the 2010 Masters.

All because of one shot. One memorable shot that will forever be a part of Masters lore as one of the greatest ever struck.

It was a 6-iron from a pine-straw lie behind two trees to the right of the par-5 13th fairway, 187 yards over Rae's Creek to the green and 207 yards to the flag that Mickelson pulled off that probably defines his career more than any shot he's ever made and any tournament he's ever won.

Mickelson had just birdied the 12th hole to take the tournament lead for the first time all week. And, as he arrived to the resting spot from his tee shot gone slightly errant, Mickelson took little time to assess his next strategic move.

"I'm going for it," he told his caddie, Jim "Bones" Mackay.

Mackay, who was known in his 25 years on Mickelson's bag as Mickelson's conscience, almost always wanted to err on the side of caution in moments like that. The two have had numerous back-and-forth conversations in the heat of battle about which shot to take, Mickelson always wanting to take the bold chance and Mackay always trying to rein him in.

Nothing was going to change Mickelson's mind on this shot, though.

Years later, recounting the shot and its magnitude, Mickelson said, "That was one of those moments, I remember having a conversation [with Mackay] as I was standing over the shot and being asked for the fourth time, 'Are you sure you want to do this?' And finally saying, 'Look, at some point you're going to have to make a great shot if you want to win.'

"And this was that moment. Sometimes you just have to clutch up and hit the shot and pull something off, pull off a tough shot. It wasn't a hard shot, but the penalty if I missed it was going to be severe. It was going to hit a tree or it was going to go into the water."

Mackay said the shot "was much scarier in person," adding, "The gap in the trees was much smaller than it looked like on TV. It was about the width of a box of a dozen balls I would say. The thing I was concerned about was there was a lot of pine straw and you could lose your footing. If you lose your footing, who knows where the ball is going to go?

"Phil let me know almost right away, 'I'm going for it here. When the green clears in front of us I'm going.'"

Mackay, trying to lay out every scenario to his man, reminded Mickelson, "Don't forget when you made all the eagles [in Saturday's third round] on 13, 14, and almost 15, don't forget that pitch shot you made.

"I was basically saying if it comes to you laying up here, you're as likely or more likely to get up and down and make four as anybody in the tournament," Mackay recalled. "He said, 'No, I'm absolutely going for this.' So, I backed off and waited for the green to clear."

As they waited, Mackay had gotten word from a TV person that K.J. Choi, who was playing in the group ahead, had just bogeyed the 13th hole to fall two strokes behind Mickelson, which prompted Mackay to say to Mickelson, "Hey, let me throw this at you. You're the boss, but does this change the way you're going to approach this shot given the fact that you are tied for the lead now?"

Mickelson's response is something that will be burned in Mackey's memory forever.

"He looked at me and said, 'Let me tell you something. If I am going to win this tournament today, I am going to have to hit a really good shot under a lot of pressure at some point. I am going to do it right now,'" Mackay recalled. "That was my entrée to get out of the way and watch him do his thing. And he hit arguably the greatest shot of his career. You almost knew he was going to hit a great shot based simply on the way he said what he said."

What does Mackay remember most about the actual shot?

"The great thing about that shot for me was the sound," he said. "The second he hit it, he hit it so pure that we knew it was going to carry."

Nick Faldo, the three-time Masters winner now in the CBS broadcast booth, told viewers, "That was the greatest shot of his life."

Mickelson, always as much a scientist as a swashbuckler, explained, "That year I did a lot of blind testing with Dave Pelz [a short game guru] to try to get my swing grooved and not see where the ball goes so that you don't make adjustments. You get every club dialed in. Well, I couldn't see that shot. Even though from behind the ball you could see the pin, standing where a left hander was standing all I saw was a tree trunk. And it took me right back to that blind test where it said, 'Trust your swing. Just make a good swing. I know this 6-iron goes straight, just make a good swing.' That's all I tried to do.

"I think that's what happens in majors. You have to go back to your practice sessions to get you through it. And that was the one...at the highest stage, too."

Mickelson would later joke with reporters after his victory that "the gap [between the trees] wasn't huge, but it was big enough, you know, for a ball to fit through."

When a reporter asked Mickelson to explain the difference between a "great shot" and a "smart shot," he said, "A great shot is when you pull it off. A smart shot is when you don't have the guts to try it."

That sentiment surprised no one close to Mickelson.

"That's him; that's how he's built," Mackay said. "He plays completely without fear. He's absolutely convinced he can pull off every shot. He wouldn't want to play any other way."

Steve Loy, Mickelson's former college coach at Arizona State and longtime manager, echoed Mackay's sentiments, saying, "That's Phil. The weaker players are always utilizing that kind of thinking as, 'I'm not going to beat myself.' He'd rather be bold enough to have the courage to do what most people can't."

Lee Westwood, who was Mickelson's playing partner in that final round, marveled at what he saw.

"It's really one of the few shots that only Phil could pull off," Westwood said. "It was a high-tariff shot. I think most people would have just chipped that one out. But, you know, that's what great players do—pull off great shots at the right time. I knew that he fancied having a go at it and that's Phil's personality and game. He's that kind of player. That's what everybody wants to see. That's why everybody likes watching him."

Mickelson didn't drain the short eagle putt, but he settled for birdie on 13 and he followed that with two more birdies on the final six holes and won by three shots.

"His life changed when he made the putt on 18 at Augusta in 2004," Mackay said of Mickelson's first Masters victory. "But [the shot at 13] was the best shot I've ever seen him hit."

When it was all over and Mickelson, showered with cheers from the packed gallery, walked off the 18th hole, he spotted his wife, Amy, who had been battling breast cancer. The medications she was on had weakened her to the point where he was not sure she'd be able to get to Augusta.

They embraced for what seemed like an eternity as the golf world looked on with tears.

"It had been an emotional year, and I was very proud of her fight and struggle she'd been through, and to come out on top in that tournament was very emotional," Mickelson said. "I don't normally shed tears over wins, and when Amy and I hugged off 18 that was a very emotional moment for us and something that I'll look back on and just cherish.

"She came in for the weekend. It was not even quite a year [since the diagnosis], but we had gotten through some of the worst stuff and that was the most emotional because of all the things we had been going through. Golf, being able to play and be on a golf course, was kind a reprieve from some of the stuff that was going on. It was more relaxing for me, and I ended up playing well that week."

The Forgotten Green Jacket

Because of the drama associated with Mickelson's 2004 win, his first major championship victory, and his 2010 win, defined by that shot on 13, his 2006 Masters win is probably the least memorable of the three—the proverbial middle child.

But it happened to come in the middle of perhaps the hottest playing stretch of his career. That '06 Masters was Mickelson's third major championship victory in nine starts, and second in a row after having won the 2005 PGA Championship. In fact, he fell just short in that final-hole collapse at Winged Foot in 2006 of capturing three consecutive majors.

Mickelson, with four birdies in his final-round 69, won that Masters by two shots over Tim Clark, who holed out from the right bunker on the 72nd hole.

Five players—Tiger Woods, two-time Masters winner José María Olazábal, Retief Goosen, Fred Couples, and Chad Campbell—tied for third place, three shots behind Mickelson.

"When I look back on it, I think what I'm most proud of is that I didn't let other people back in it," Mickelson said. "They had to come and chase me down and make birdies to do it."

Mickelson had come into that '06 Masters on a tear, a week removed from winning the BellSouth Classic in Atlanta by 13 shots at 28-under par.

"The only year that I really knew going in that I was most likely going to win was in '06, because I had just won by 13 the week before and I felt like I was playing so good that if I just carried anywhere near close to that level I was going to have a good week," Mickelson said. "When I won in '04, I always knew I would win, but I never knew when it was going to happen. I had a good feeling about that week in the sense that I just kind of believed that I was going to win, but I didn't know it the way I knew it in '06.

"I had a good feeling about that tournament, I knew I was playing well, I knew I was prepared, but I still had to execute."

With Augusta lengthening the golf course 155 yards for that 2006 Masters, Mickelson went with the unconventional strategy of using two drivers that year—one for a draw and the other for a fade—and he ended up leading the field in average driving distance.

"It was a huge help," Mickelson recalled. "I got 20, 25 more yards with the driver that draws."

He'd experimented with the two drivers the week before in Atlanta and it worked out well.

"I'd like to say one thing about the changes," Mickelson, ever the tinkerer, said. "I like them."

A big edge for Mickelson in the final round was that his playing partner was Couples, one of his good friends in the game. That proved to be a highly advantageous pairing for him.

"I love playing with Fred," Mickelson said. "We had a great time and we kept saying how lucky we were to be in the final pairing on Sunday at the Masters, and how much fun it was. It made for a very fun day. We were pulling for each other to make some birdies and encouraging each other. I felt this great feeling of accomplishment to be able to beat guys like Tiger and Retief and Ernie [Els] and Vijay [Singh] and Fred and some incredible and talented players."

After taking a one-shot lead into that final round, Mickelson carried a three-shot lead up the 18th fairway and reveled in the "stress-free" walk.

Spikegate

For all the pleasant memorable experiences Mickelson has had at Augusta, there was one that took place in the 2005 tournament that he'd rather forget: some contentious moments with Vijay Singh, who'd complained in the middle of the second round that the spikes in Mickelson's golf shoes were leaving marks on the greens.

Singh sent a rules official to Mickelson's group in the middle of the round to measure Mickelson's spikes, infuriating the usually affable Mickelson.

That led to an explosive incident that escalated into an animated shouting match between Mickelson and Singh when they bumped into each other in the Champions Locker Room during a weather delay later on.

Singh, the No. 1 player in the world at the time, delivered what one player called "a completely classless" move of "clear gamesmanship" when he complained to a Masters referee about Mickelson's spikes during the Friday completion of the first round.

Singh, playing in the group behind Mickelson, summoned a referee at the 12th hole, where he was playing at the time, and complained that Mickelson's spikes were leaving large spike marks in the green.

"He said on the 12th hole that someone in the group in front was tracking the green with his shoes," PGA Tour rules official

Steve Rintoul said. "When he looked at where the track was going, he figured out it was Phil."

Mickelson hit his tee shot down the left side of the 13th fairway, and a rules official met him off the tee. Mickelson showed him his soles, one then the other. Rintoul said another official on the 13th green watched for abnormal footprints and found there was no problem.

According to Joe Damiano, the caddie for Stuart Appleby, Mickelson's playing partner in the round, the referee told Mickelson another official was going to be sent out to "file down" his spikes, causing Appleby to crack, "What are they going to send? A blacksmith?"

The official with a file was never sent out and Mickelson continued playing in his own size 12 Callaway shoes.

According to Damiano, Mickelson remained outwardly calm about the odd inquiry as he played out his first round. But, Damiano said the Singh complaint infuriated Mickelson, the defending Masters champion.

Mickelson later walked into the locker room and saw Singh sitting at a table with fellow player Mark O'Meara, and said Singh asked if he'd like Mickelson to take him outside and "kick his ass."

Mickelson, trying to downplay the incident, said, "I was extremely distracted and would have appreciated if it would have been handled differently or after the round. After sitting in the locker room for a while, I heard Vijay talking to other players about it and I confronted him. He expressed his concerns. I expressed my disappointment with the way it was handled.

"Given the wet and slippery conditions, more than a third of the field is using steel spikes. And I make every effort to tap down whatever spike marks I leave."

Mickelson was wearing metal eight-millimeter spikes in his golf shoes, which is commonplace, though many players had gone to plastic soft spikes by then.

Appleby was shocked by Singh, saying, "You never do something like that in the middle of a round. That's something you take up with the player after the round is over."

He also chided Singh, the 2001 Masters champion, for not having the "guts" to speak to Mickelson one-to-one about the issue.

He suggested Singh, who was 2-under at the time and just coming off a bogey at No. 11, recognized Mickelson, who was 3-under at the time, was playing well so he was obviously trying to throw him off his game.

According to Will Nicholson, the chairman of the Masters competition committee, there was "no ruling" and Mickelson's spikes were within the rules.

"We got a call, and how it got labeled onto Phil I have no idea," Nicholson said. "There was some spike that apparently tore up some grass, and Phil was the one that was blamed. One of our officials talked to Phil to see if there was a burr on the side of one of his spikes. He very generously, as you know he would, said he would change them if there was a problem. There wasn't."

Of course, in Sunday's final round, Mickelson and Singh were paired together in a tension-packed twosome. Not surprisingly, neither played well as Tiger Woods went on to win his fourth green jacket.

Singh finished one stroke better than Mickelson, whose 74 included double bogeys on the par-3 12th and 16th holes that ended his quest to win back-to-back Masters.

After the round, Singh refused to address the Spikegate incident and Mickelson refused to blame his poor performance on the distraction of the unfortunate pairing.

"That stuff was not a factor at all," Mickelson said.

Then, almost tongue-in-cheek, Mickelson said of himself and Singh, "We had a great day. We had a great time. We laughed. We giggled. We had a great time. It was a fun day."

For sure, he'd had better days at the Masters, and there, too, were more to come.

PART SIX

SATURDAY

Chapter 17

THE GREEN JACKET

It's not the most fashionable garment you've ever seen. It's not even worth that much money, believed to be valued at about $250. It's just a green jacket. And who wears green jackets, anyway?

Augusta National members do. So do Masters champions.

The green jacket is to golf what the Lombardi Trophy is to the NFL or the Stanley Cup is to the NHL. It's the pinnacle of awards for golfers, the most iconic trophy in the sport.

The Pantone 342–colored green jacket was first awarded to Masters winners in 1949, the 15th Masters. Augusta National members were the first to wear the green jacket; it was introduced as a means for members of the public to spot them amongst the crowd during tournament week.

Bobby Jones, the co-designer of Augusta National, attended a dinner at Royal Liverpool Golf Club where club captains were all wearing matching club jackets. That's where the idea of the green jackets was born.

The first were bought from Brooks Uniform Company in New York, but the members found them to be uncomfortable, made of too-thick material.

Since 1967, the jackets have been made by Hamilton Tailoring Company out of Cincinnati, with the tropical-weight wool material sourced from Dublin, Georgia. The brass buttons are made in Massachusetts. The breast-pocket patch, with the club's logo, is sewn in North Carolina.

The jacket belonging to the winner of the first ever tournament, Horton Smith in 1934, was sold at auction by family members for $600,000.

Each Masters winner is given a jacket. Regardless of how many Masters they've won, though, they have one jacket, and it resides in their locker at the club. For example, Jack Nicklaus has won a record six Masters, but he doesn't have six green jackets.

Green jacket holders are forbidden from taking them from the grounds of Augusta National. The only exception is the current winner, and he can only have it off the premises for the year after he's won it.

Tournament winners are given a temporary jacket when they win before having a customized fit delivered in the weeks following their victory. Then they're required to return it to the club upon their return to defend the title.

Gary Player is the only player to have broken the rule. After his 1961 win, Player returned from South Africa with his green jacket and then lost in a playoff to Arnold Palmer in 1962 and went back home with it to South Africa.

"I win the tournament and I assume when they put the jacket on you, that's your jacket," Player said. "I'm so excited; I leave and I go home to South Africa with the jacket. Three days later, I hear this call, 'Gary, this is Clifford Roberts here.' I said, 'I hope you're not calling me reverse charges,' because you know, you had to make him laugh a little bit because he was quite a dour man. He said, 'I believe, Gary, you've taken the jacket home to South Africa.'

"I said, 'I did, Mr. Roberts.' He said, 'Nobody ever takes the jacket off these grounds whatsoever.' So, I thought very quickly, and I said, 'Mr. Roberts, if you want it, come and fetch it.' He saw the lighter side of things and he said, 'Please don't ever wear it in public.'

"It's not like today. If you win today, you can wear it in public for one year. That didn't apply then. I put a plastic cover over it and never used it again until I came back."

Nicklaus joked, "Can you imagine in those days Clifford Roberts going to South Africa to fetch Gary's jacket?"

"Only a 40-hour flight in those days with no jets," Player joked.

Tom Watson recalled the first time he won the Masters, in 1977, the jacket he received wasn't his size of 42 regular. Augusta National usually sizes up potential champions, but instead gave him a 46 long. "They didn't assess my size very well," Watson said. "It didn't matter to me."

Nicklaus, too, had a size snafu. His first was a 46 long and his size is 43 regular.

"The next year when I came back, they didn't ask me to go get a jacket, never mentioned my jacket," Nicklaus recalled. "Tom Dewey had a jacket, former governor who lost to Truman in the presidency. His jacket fit me, and I wore his jacket for probably 15 years, maybe longer. Nobody ever mentioned, 'Do you have your green jacket?' I had Tom Dewey's. I never got a green jacket. Finally, I won six Masters and still nobody had ever given me a green jacket.

"I told the story to [then club chairman] Jack Stephens in 1998 and Jack Stephens said, 'What? You've never been given a green jacket?' I said, 'No. Nobody's ever mentioned it.' So, I got back the week of the tournament and he says, 'You will go down to the pro shop and you will be fit for your green jacket,' which is the one I wear now."

Tiger Woods, writing about his 1997 Masters win in his book *Unprecedented: The Masters and Me*, recalled: "After much celebration, I fell asleep fully clothed and hugging the green jacket like a blanket."

Over the years, some players have had some fun with the jacket in their year as champion. Sergio García, the 2017 winner, seemingly wore it every place he went.

"If I told you everywhere I took it, I will probably miss my tee time on Thursday," García joked when he returned to Augusta in 2018.

The most important place García wore the jacket was at his wedding to Angela Akins three months after his victory.

He also wore it to the "El Clasico" soccer match between Real Madrid and Barcelona, to Wimbledon for a Rafael Nadal match, to the New York Stock Exchange, and to numerous television studios for numerous guest appearances.

At one of the TV appearances, he hugged a stagehand who apparently had oil or grease on his shirt, which stained the jacket. "I'm thinking, 'My God, I've had the jacket for a day-and-a-half and I already have two massive stains on it,'" García recalled, saying he took it to a dry cleaner. "I think people know I've worn it and I don't like to show off and wear it left and right. At the end of the day, you've got to respect how iconic the jacket is. It's not just a piece of clothing. It means so much more than that. You have to be very respectful of it and wear it when you should, not all the time."

Jordan Spieth, the 2015 winner, recalled the feeling he had once he realized the jacket was his to wear for the year.

"It's once you leave the property, that's when it really hits you," Spieth said. "When you stand on the green it's one thing, but you're kind of thinking about what you want to say and how you want to thank everybody who made it possible. It's not until I left the property that I truly kind of felt what it was like to wear the jacket, and wear the jacket I did, for a year. It didn't leave my side."

Phil Mickelson was photographed wearing the jacket to a Krispy Kreme doughnut drive-thru in 2010. He, too, once joked that he would put the jacket in his golf bag and pull it out if it was chilly on the course.

Three-time winner Mickelson, ever the needler and practical jokester to friends, said, "I wouldn't carry three jackets around with me but I would say, 'I've got two more, if you're cold as well.'"

Patrick Reed, the 2018 winner, was asked about his favorite memory with the jacket.

"It would have had to have been right after we won and right after I got done talking in the press conference, right after we finished," he recalled. "I went back to Butler Cabin, and my daughter was there, and she just came over and gave me a big hug and told me I did it and told me she loved me. That is by far the best experience I've ever had with the green jacket.

"That's a memory and a moment that I'll never forget, no matter if I were to win multiple other green jackets. It's going to be hard to be able to top a moment like that that I was able to cherish with the little one."

He did have a funny exchange while wearing the jacket to a Knicks game at Madison Square Garden.

"It was on a Monday night, [my wife] Justine and I were at the Knicks game and were sitting courtside for the first time," Reed recalled. "I had Chris Rock right next to us. A couple seats down is 2 Chainz. He just kind of keeps looking down, and you can tell he's kind of looking down like, 'All right, this isn't the normal guy that sits in these seats; who is that?'

"And then when they announced me during one of the time-outs, then a couple minutes later there was a timeout and he just kind of reaches over, and he kind of touches the jacket, and he goes, 'So that's the real thing, huh?' I'm like, 'Yes, sir, yes, it is.' It's pretty cool to see just kind of the wide variety of people no matter what their background is, no matter what their age is or anything, how many people recognize the green jacket. I just think it's such a cool thing how many people recognize what the green jacket is and what it actually stands for."

The massive oak tree that sits between the iconic white clubhouse and the first tee is the oldest living member of Augusta National. *(Oliver Katcher)*

For many people, the Par-3 Contest held on the Wednesday before the Masters each year is more notable than the tournament itself. *(Oliver Katcher)*

The 1997 Masters was Tiger Woods' first as a professional. Needless to say, it would not be his last. *(AP Images)*

Arnold Palmer has the iconic green jacket draped over his shoulders by Jack Nicklaus after winning the 1964 Masters. *(AP Images)*

Mike Weir helps Phil Mickelson into his green jacket after his first Masters win in 2004. *(AP Images)*

The clubhouse at Augusta National, located near the first tee, dates back to the 1850s. *(Oliver Katcher)*

One of the first images the Masters brings to mind for many are gorgeous azaleas in full bloom. *(Oliver Katcher)*

There are so many rules and regulations surrounding the green jacket, one of the most exclusive items of clothing in the world, that few know about. *(Oliver Katcher)*

Jennifer Kupcho won the Augusta National Women's Amateur tournament in 2019. The tournament debuted in 2019. Augusta National first began admitting women as members in 2012. *(AP Images)*

The Spanish golfer known as El Niño finally got the monkey off his back in 2017 when he won his first Masters. *(AP Images)*

Rory McIlroy is still looking for his first Masters win. His best result was finishing fourth in 2015. *(AP Images)*

His victory in the 2015 Masters also happened to be Jordan Spieth's first major win. *(AP Images)*

Sergio Garcia congratulates Patrick Reed (left), 2018 Masters champion. It was Reed's first major win. *(AP Images)*

Tiger Woods' triumphant victory in the 2019 Masters made for one of the best comeback stories in sports history. *(AP Images)*

Chapter 18

THE EL NIÑO ENIGMA

Sergio García, after he shot a disappointing 75 in the third round of the 2012 Masters (in which he would finish tied for 12th), sounded a bit dead inside.

In a shocking interview with Spanish reporters, García delivered a dark analysis of his state of mind as it related to winning a major championship, something he hadn't yet accomplished.

"I'm not good enough," García said. "I don't have the thing I need to have."

When asked if he meant winning the Masters, García said, "Any major."

"In 13 years, I have come to the conclusion that I need to play for second or third place," he said. "I'm not good enough, and today I know it. I've been trying for 13 years, and I don't feel capable of winning. I don't know what happened to me. Maybe it's something psychological. I'm not good enough for the majors.

"Tell me something I can do. I had my chances and opportunities and I wasted them. I have no more options. I wasted my options."

The day after that rant, García did not back off his comments.

"Everything I say, I say it because I feel it," García said. "If I didn't mean it, I couldn't stand here and lie like a lot of the guys do. If I felt like I could win, I would do it."

Three years before his 2012 self-loathing rant to the Spanish media, García, in an interview with the Golf Channel, torched Augusta National after his final-round 74 that left him tied for 38th in 2009.

"I don't like it, to tell you the truth," García said. "I don't think it's fair. It's too tricky. Even when it's dry, you still get mud balls in the middle of the fairway. It's just too much of a guessing game."

When he was asked how he would change Augusta National, García said, "I don't care. They can do whatever. It is not my problem. I just come here, play golf, and go home."

Two days later, García's management company did its best to quell the storm he created, releasing a damage-control statement supposedly from García. It read: "Out of frustration, I blamed the golf course instead of putting the blame where it belongs, on myself. Augusta National is one of the most iconic golf courses in the game and playing in the Masters each year is an honor."

―――――

Finally, a Breakthrough

It's weird how things turn out sometimes in sports.

After years of heartbreak (and a lot of bellyaching), García, a tortured soul of sorts in major championships, finally would win one. And at Augusta National, of all places.

He'd played in 73 career major championships, 71 of them consecutively, and posted top-10 finishes in nearly a third of them, with four second places. And finally, in 2017, García won a green jacket.

Five years earlier, after yet another disappointing Masters finish, García left everyone to believe he never would win a major because he said as much, conceding he felt like he simply didn't have it in him.

And yet, there was García in the final round of the 81st Masters, putting an end to all the doubt and all the pent-up frustration, winning at the place he had grown to loathe.

García, at age 37, was a major championship winner at last, overcoming years of baggage, doubt, jangled nerves, and, ultimately, Justin Rose on the first playoff hole, a birdie on 18 the difference.

"It's been such a long time coming," an emotional García said afterward. "There's always uncertainty. But, I felt a calmness I've never felt in a major championship Sunday."

There were signs all that week that suggested it might be a different tournament for García, one that would be special.

There was a poignant Wednesday night text message from fellow Spaniard and two-time Masters winner José María Olazábal imploring him to believe in himself that buoyed García's psyche.

There was the ball he hit on the 13th hole in the third round that somehow defied gravity and clung to the steep greenside bank instead of tumbling back into Rae's Creek. He converted what would have been an almost-certain bogey into a birdie. A lucky break for García, who has spent most of his career lamenting all the bad breaks he has endured.

Then there was No. 13 in the final round, when García pulled his drive into the trees and azaleas to the left of the fairway into an unplayable lie, forcing him to take a drop and penalty shot. He already was two shots behind Rose, his chances to win on life support.

But García somehow saved par with a punch shot from the pine needles to the fairway, a wedge onto the green and one putt, while Rose missed a five-foot birdie putt that could have given him a three-shot lead.

"Funny enough, most other weeks I would have been thinking, 'Here we go again,'" García said. "Obviously, I wasn't happy. But from there, the most important thing was that I felt calm. That calmness gave me confidence. I was like: 'It's okay. You're doing everything right. You're playing great. It's your time.' I just kept believing."

Then there was García carding an eagle on the par-5 15th hole to tie Rose at 9-under. The last Masters champion to make eagle on No. 15 en route to victory? Olazábal in 1994.

Good omens were everywhere for a change for García, who has spent his life playing the victim.

And finally, there was this: the Sunday of that final round would have been the 60th birthday of Seve Ballesteros, García's lifelong idol.

The ending was awkward, and it provided a perfect canvas for García to end his major championship drought. His weakness always has been his putting, and he failed to win the tournament on the 18th hole in regulation, missing a five-foot putt for the victory, leaving it right all the way, the ball never even grazing the cup.

In 2007, García lipped out an eight-foot putt for the win on the 72nd hole of the British Open, leading to a playoff he lost to Padraig Harrington.

His miss on 18 in the final round sent García and Rose back to the 18th tee for the playoff hole that García won thanks to Rose hitting his drive into the trees to the right of the fairway.

Rose, the 2013 U.S. Open winner and a friend of García's, understandably was gutted afterward, but was gracious in defeat. "If there was anyone to lose to, it would be Sergio," he said.

"He's had his fair share of heartbreak. It's nice for him now to have that monkey off his back, and I was very pleased for him."

To illustrate how far gone García's belief had gotten, you needed only to go back to those words after that 2012 Masters when asked if he thought he ever would win a major.

So much for that. A Masters hater had become a lover of Augusta National over the course of those four magical days in April 2017.

How did it happen?

Perhaps not without García meeting—and marrying—Angela Akins, who, by the accounts of those who know García well and other close observers, imbued him with a sense of belief.

"Angela is a good woman," said Danny Willett, the 2016 Masters champion who had the honor of slipping the green jacket over García's shoulders. "He has had a lot of years of heartache on the course and a little bit off it and he has found someone there who he loves and enjoys. It does make a difference. To have the stability off the course, it definitely does help you on the course."

Irishman and former Ryder Cup teammate Padraig Harrington said, "It's Angela who has been a big difference to him. I saw it in the team room at the last Ryder Cup (in 2016). When he holed the winning putt, she didn't come running on to the green. She waited to let him enjoy it. She is the big driving force."

Fellow Irishman Paul McGinley said he thinks Akins "has added the extra vital dimension" for García, adding, "It's not like he was miles away; he was just one percent away from being a major champion. She has that bit of steeliness about her, and I think that has permeated through to Sergio. There is a good team behind him, a real belief, and with the monkey off his back I wouldn't be surprised if it led to major number two, three, or even four."

Akins' father, Marty, is a former All-American college quarter-back, and her grandfather was Ray Akins, a legendary high school football coach who was also the grandfather of New Orleans Saints quarterback Drew Bees. So there's some athletic strength in her family—strength that has seemingly permeated into García's competitive soul.

"They've definitely helped, there's no doubt the whole family has," García said after his Masters win. "Marty is a very, very positive, very, you know, outspoken and a very, very confident kind of guy. Angela is the same way. They are all very competitive.

"It's quite simple: when good people are telling you things you need to get better at, and they are telling you from their hearts, you listen, and that's what I did. Sometimes they tell me things I don't want to hear and it's not easy, because I know how much of a hard-headed man I can be. But it's been great.

"I didn't think I would be able to change this quickly, but I'm glad I did. It turned out to be an amazing week in a place I love but where I've had some tough times. To be able to deal with those emotions and accept the good and bad things was something that definitely gives me a sense of extra pride."

García credited his support system for helping carry him through some stressful moments in the final round of that '17 Masters—like when he bogeyed the 10th and 11th and then drove his tee shot into the trees at the par-five 13th.

"I was very calm, much calmer than I've felt in probably any major championship on Sunday," García said. "In the past at 13, I would have said to my caddie, 'Why doesn't it go through?' But I was like, 'If that's what's supposed to happen, let it happen. Let's try to make a great 5 here and see if we can put in a hell of a finish to have a chance.'"

García recalled a moment after one of his several disappointments at Augusta when 2009 Masters champion Ángel Cabrera offered him words of encouragement.

"Cabrera and I, we get along nicely, [and] he just kind of put his arm around me and said, 'You know, just keep going, don't worry about it, these things happen. If you keep going the way you're going, you'll be fine. You'll manage to get through one day.'"

No Defense

García's defense of the green jacket he won in 2017 is not so memorable. He finished in a tie for last place, oddly enough, with Willett, the 2016 champion.

What made García's 2018 Masters memorable for all the wrong reasons was *how* he flamed out in his title defense. He hit his five balls in the water on the par-5 15th hole en route to shooting an opening-round 81.

He took a 13 on the hole, ballooning his score at the time from 2-over-par to 10-over. His 13 tied Tommy Nakajima (1978, hole No. 15) and Tom Weiskopf (1980, No. 12) as the highest individual score on a hole in Masters history. Amazingly, García sank a nine-foot putt to avoid the 14 to own the record for highest score ever himself.

"It's the first time in my career where I make a 13 without missing a shot, simple as that," García said. "I felt like I hit a lot of good shots, and unfortunately the ball just didn't want to stop."

García's 81 was followed by a second-round 78 and an early-exit missed cut—though he had to stick around for the weekend to slip the green jacket over the next winner's shoulders, as is a part of the annual Masters ceremony.

"I'm disappointed and I would have loved to have had a better defense of my title," García said. "Unfortunately, this is golf, and sometimes that's what happens."

García, who named his daughter Azalea Adele in honor of his Masters victory and an ode to the name of the 13th hole at Augusta National, tweeted the day after his nightmare on No. 15 that year: "What happened on 15 yesterday was unfortunate for me and it hurt but I tried to handle it like a Masters champion should. That same hole gave me that green jacket last year so we might end up naming our next kid Firethorn."

Firethorn is the name of Augusta's 15th hole, which swallowed those five balls of García's and doomed him to the highest two-round total (159) ever posted by a defending Masters champion. It's also the hole where García hit an 8-iron that clipped the flag and set up a 12-foot eagle putt to tie him for the lead en route to his Masters victory the year before.

His week as defending champion was hardly the week García was expecting.

"I've talked to José María [Olazábal], and he told me when you get there and you go through the gates and drive down Magnolia Lane as a Masters champion...he couldn't explain the feeling, but he said, 'You'll just see it feels different,'" García said. "To walk around the grounds at Augusta and wearing the jacket and being seen as Masters champion and everything...it's just so different."

García's year following his Masters victory had been storybook. He married Akins and they had their daughter.

"I feel very proud for being able to win a major, and to win the Masters on top of that," García said. "But you know, like what they all tell me: 'Has it changed your life?' I don't think and I don't feel like it has. I'm still doing the same things. It's something that until it happens, you don't know what it's going to feel like and what it's going to do to you. But on my regard, I'm happy that I don't feel it has changed me. I don't feel like I'm better than I was before."

Akins, whom García met when she was working at the Golf Channel, has served as a massive positive force in his life.

"I remember a year before the [2017] Masters, being at Augusta with Sergio and talking about particular things that I thought he should work on," Akins recalled in 2018. "I remember he was talking about how somebody had gotten lucky and he had gotten unlucky. We talked about how you can't control that. You're just wasting your energy. He's gotten so much better than that. In golf, you get bad breaks all the time. And you get good breaks."

Chapter 19

THE BIG EASY

The list isn't a long one, but there have been a fair number of players who never fell in love with Augusta National and the Masters over the years.

One of the most prominent of those was Ernie Els, the affable South African, who had several near-misses trying to win a green jacket in his 23 attempts without reward and finally left with a bad taste in his mouth. Els had two runner-up finishes, edged out by Tiger Woods in 2000 and Phil Mickelson in 2004. In all, he posted six finishes in the top 8.

Before the 2019 Masters, which he had not qualified for, Els was resigned to the fact that he'd never get to play a 24th Masters and considered the venerable tournament dead to him.

"To be honest with you, I won't miss the place," Els said. "I had enough of it—especially the last five years I played it terribly."

Els' most recent results at Augusta at that time were, indeed, dodgy. He'd finished 53rd in 2017 after shooting 83–78 on the weekend. In 2016, he missed the cut after shooting 80–73. He had a missed cut in 2014 sandwiched between a tie for 22nd in 2015 and a tie for 13th in 2013. In 2012, he didn't even qualify to get into the field.

Els' theory is simply that some players at Augusta have been treated better by the golf gods than others.

"You can be on that curve—and I think Mickelson and Tiger and Freddie [Couples] are on that curve—and then you have me and [Tom] Weiskopf and [Greg] Norman on the other curve," Els said.

Mickelson, Woods, and Couples, who got that famous break in 1992 en route to winning when his ball somehow stayed on the grassy bank at No. 12 and didn't trickle into Rae's Creek in the final round, always seem to have had positive memories at Augusta.

Els—like Norman and Weiskopf, who also never won despite heartbreaking close calls—not so much.

"When a thing stings you it keeps stinging you," Els said. "When it gives to you it keeps on giving. I've seen that with Gary Player. I've seen it with Jack [Nicklaus]. I've got a love-hate relationship with the place. It was always almost like a curse to me. It was not a romantic deal to me. It was a fucking nightmare for the most part.

"Then," Els went on, "you start disliking the place when you shouldn't. I try to keep my honor for the golf course and the people, because the members are great and the course is actually great. But it just doesn't want to give me anything and then I was finally like, 'You know what? That's fine. Let's move on.'

"It's like, 'Shit, it's not giving me anything. How many times do you want to run into a wall?' That's how I felt my last couple of years. I didn't want to say it before, and I don't have any bad feelings about it. It's just the way it is. I had enough of it. Move on. It's a unique place, but I'm done with it. It's done with me."

The shame of this is that Els had some brilliant runs at the green jacket. He lost to Mickelson in one of the most epic Sunday back-nine duels in tournament history. His final-round 67 wasn't enough as Mickelson shot 30 on the back nine and won his first career major.

"I don't really have any Masters highlights," Els said. "I guess the final round in '04 was a highlight. I'm just glad that I had the experience that Nicklaus and Phil and Tiger and all the great Masters players had in that I was in the mix once, I mean really in the heat of it. That Sunday was phenomenal. It was one of the best ever. It was obviously a huge disappointment to me, but when I look back now, at least I can say that I was in the mix when the crowds were going nuts. I was hitting good shots and my opponents are hitting good shots."

Els' most embarrassing moment came in 2016, when he took a record nine on the first hole in the opening round. En route to that stunning number, Els six-putted from two feet.

"I can't explain it," Els said after shooting 80 that day. "It's unexplainable. I couldn't get the putter back. I was standing there and I've got a three-footer. I've made thousands of three-footers. And I just couldn't take it back. And then I just kind of lost count. I tried to fight. I don't know how I stayed out there [and finished]."

Els, who'd been battling the putting yips at that time in his career, made a reference to having "snakes" in his head.

"It's the first time ever I've seen anything like that," Jason Day, Els' playing partner for those first two rounds, said. "I feel for Ernie. I've known Ernie for a long time now. I didn't realize he was fighting stuff like that upstairs with the putter. You just don't want to see any player go through that."

The quintuple-bogey is the highest score on the first hole in Masters history, surpassing the 8s taken by Olin Browne and Scott Simpson in 1998, Billy Casper in 2001, and Jeev Milkha Singh in 2007.

Tom Watson once 5-putted the 16th green at Augusta. Seve Ballesteros is famous for his quote following a 4-putt at a Masters years ago. When he was asked to describe how he 4-putted, he said, "I miss, I miss, I miss, I make."

As a credit to Els, he powered on and didn't quit the round, something the likes of John Daly might have done.

"I don't know how I stayed out there," he said. "But you love the game and you've got to have respect for the tournament and so forth. The last thing you want to do is do that on a golf course."

The next day, Els said he walked to the practice range to warm up for the second round and could see pity in people's faces.

"It was a very weird, surreal feeling," said Els, who shot 73 in the second round and missed the cut. "I walked on to the range and even the players and caddies, they kind of just looked at me as if I don't have pants on or something, or like I stole something. But they've got a good reason to look at me funny for what happened. [That first hole] was just absolutely nightmarish. After what I did you feel quite embarrassed."

Els' odd meltdown was reminiscent of some athletes in other sports who had their own form of the yips.

Former New York Mets catcher Mackey Sasser was once unable to throw the ball back to the pitcher without pumping his fist into his glove several times. That led to base runners stealing bases in bunches, leading to Sasser eventually having to quit the game.

Former New York Yankees second baseman Chuck Knoblauch, in the '90s, lost his ability to throw to first base. Knoblauch, once a Gold Glove fielder, lost his career to the weird affliction.

St. Louis Cardinals pitcher Rick Ankiel suffered a mental and physical meltdown in the 2000 playoffs, throwing a series of wild pitches. It affected him so profoundly that he was never able to find the strike zone again and had to quit pitching. Ankiel went to the minor leagues and tried to make it as an outfielder.

Returning to golf, Tiger Woods went through the chipping yips, seemingly related to his back ailments. It led to a stunning 82 in the second round of the 2015 Waste Management Phoenix Open.

If Woods, arguably the greatest golfer ever, can get the yips, then nobody is immune.

Els was warmed by the reaction he got from the spectators in the wake of his nightmare.

"The patrons were great toward me," he said. "I appreciate that. You play long enough, you make a fool of yourself somewhere, but I did it on the biggest stage. But I'll take something out of this. I'll sit down and see where we go."

Els said he'd been "working on something" with his short putting stroke that "backfired" on that opening hole.

"I was trying some new stuff—can you believe it?—from Tuesday onwards [and] I thought it might be something in the right direction, but obviously it wasn't," he said. "Maybe I felt like that because my brain [was] telling me, 'This is not normal' and [it] just went haywire."

Els said he went back to his rented house the night after the first round. "I think we were all still in shock, the whole household. We just weren't saying much, and I had my dinner and watched the NBA game, Miami against Chicago. Just kind of shell-shocked. I slept okay, and then [Friday] morning I felt very bad when I got to the course. You feel weird. People kind of give you a funny look, not the normal look. I was feeling down, really down. I felt kind of embarrassed. I didn't feel like myself."

Perhaps the most poignant moment of the entire affair came after Els' first round. *Augusta Chronicle* golf writer Scott Michaux bumped into Els in the clubhouse grill and asked him, "How you holding up?"

"I'm a little dead inside," Els responded.

Chapter 20

THE PROTEST

Martha Burk doesn't play golf.
    She never had any ambition to become a member of Augusta National.

But she'll go down as one of the most influential figures in the history of Augusta National in that she helped open the club's doors to female members.

It was a well-publicized campaign in 2002 and 2003 to get the most exclusive golf club on the planet to invite women into its membership orchestrated by Burk, a leader of the National Council of Women's Organizations, that helped elicit change.

Burk waged a very public battle with William "Hootie" Johnson, then the chairman of Augusta National. It was a battle that elicited some colorful and defiant trash talk. It was a battle that led to a demonstration in a muddy field just down Washington Road from Magnolia Lane on the Saturday of the 2003 Masters that turned into an embarrassing sideshow with the KKK and an Elvis impersonator showing up and more reporters present than demonstrators on hand.

But it was a battle that—in either a big way or a little—helped open Magnolia Lane to at least some female members.

The Impetus

It all began on April 11, 2002, when Burk read a newspaper article quoting Johnson saying, "We have no exclusionary policies as far as our membership is concerned."

Burk, on behalf of the NCWO, sent a nine-sentence letter to Johnson demanding that he "open [his] membership to women now, so that this is not an issue when the tournament is staged next year."

Johnson's public response turned out to be a wildly ill-advised move that became a public relations fiasco for the club.

"We do not intend to become a trophy in their display case," Johnson ranted in a response letter to Burk. "There may well come a day when women will be invited to join our membership but that timetable will be ours, and not at the point of a bayonet. I have found your letter's several references to discrimination, allusions to sponsors and your setting of deadlines to be both offensive and coercive. Any further communication between us would not be productive."

Johnson's outrage to Burk's letter ignited a national debate and, eventually, the demonstration Burk engineered. It was a demonstration that cost the city of Augusta $120,000 in a settlement after a Circuit Court of Appeals later agreed that Burk's rights had been violated when her group was forced to protest in that muddy field away from the club instead of outside the gates of Augusta National.

Following the Burk–Johnson public bruhaha, two of the Masters' major corporate sponsors—Coca-Cola and IBM—along

with its broadcast partner, CBS, and the PGA Tour, issued statements shying away from the topic by saying that it is inappro-
priate for them to comment on Augusta's membership policies.

"I don't think it's for us to be concerned about," then–PGA
Tour commissioner Tim Finchem said. "We don't have a contractual
obligation with Augusta National."

The matter took an explosive turn on July 16, 2002, when
Tiger Woods, in a pre-tournament press conference at the British
Open at Muirfield, was asked about Augusta National's exclusion-
ary policy preventing female members.

"[Augusta National is] entitled to set up their own rules the
way they want them," Woods said. "That's the way they want
to set it up. It's their prerogative to set it up that way. It would
be nice to see everyone have an equal chance to participate if
they wanted to, but there is nothing you can do about it...it's
just the way it is."

Woods' words were shocking considering that his early existence in golf was all about opening doors to those who were
excluded because of prejudice, emphasized by his first Nike TV
commercial that blared against his exclusion from certain golf
clubs because of the color of his skin.

The immediate fallout was a front-page column in the *New
York Post* with a large block-letter headline screaming HYPOCRITE
ripping him for being "gutless" with his "straddle-the-fence
answer" to the question about women not being allowed as members of Augusta National.

Woods' stature in the game, as not only the best player in
the world but probably the most recognized golfer on the planet,
was such that he could have made a difference if he wanted to.
Yet, intensely protective and careful about his image, this was
the greatest example of all on how he constantly refused to take
public stands on any issues.

"I find it shocking and appalling that somebody who has brought so much stature to the game of golf is basically saying it's all right to discriminate against humans," Charles Farrell, the director of Rainbow Sports, a division of Jesse Jackson's Rainbow Push Wall Street Project for expanded opportunities for minorities (including women) in the sports industry, told *The Post* in that column.

"When he first turned pro, his whole TV [commercial] campaign was about the places that wouldn't let him play because of race. That was very dramatic and very effective, and there were some clubs that had excluded blacks that opened doors to blacks because of the pressure that came from [Woods'] comments.

"To condone discriminating against women I think plays right into the hands of those who would want things back the way they were before 1954," continued Farrell. "Tiger Woods has brought such enormity to the game of golf that his comments to the negative side of this sets us back 20 to 30 years. It's very disappointing to see a person of color represent that kind of thinking."

Farrell said he was certain that if Woods took a stand and even threatened to pull out of a tournament played at a club where women were excluded, those clubs would open to women members in a hurry.

Woods, a three-time Masters winner at Augusta, was asked at that time if, with his stature in the game, he could force a change.

"I've done my part so far trying to get more kids who haven't been able to have access to the game; that's what my foundation is about," he said.

Farrell countered, "I see a lot of those kids at his [Tiger Woods Foundation] clinics are young girls. What kind of message is he sending to those young girls who are coming up and saying,

'I want to be like Tiger?' To condemn them to a second-class golf citizenship I think is absurd. It's very sad."

Woods, who is of African American and Asian descent, was asked if he felt this discrimination against women also applies to African Americans and Asians.

"Yes, I do," he said.

It seemed alarming that the most influential person in sports had allowed himself to acquiesce to the blatant discrimination and simply pass it off with such an ignorant default statement that amounted to, "It is what it is."

Woods' statement infuriated Burk, who quickly responded.

"Tiger Woods is uniquely positioned to help make changes and should reconsider his notion that nothing can be done," Burk told the *Washington Post*.

"We will not take the view that some have, [that] Tiger has spoken and now it's over," Burk said in an interview with the *New York Times*. "It is not over. For all my respect for him, Tiger is naive when it comes to changing course."

Several weeks later, Woods resorted to damage control with a statement he released on his website, tigerwoods.com. It read: "Would I like to see women members? Yes, that would be great, but I am only one voice. Everyone has to understand that Augusta isn't quick to change. No matter what I or the press says, they do things at their own pace...and won't buckle to outside pressure."

With pressure mounting from Burk's crusade, which included letters to the Masters corporate sponsors, Johnson announced on August 30, 2002, that the tournament was dropping its three sponsors—Citigroup, Coca-Cola, and IBM—and would telecast the 2003 tournament commercial-free. That, according to reports, cost the club an estimated $20 million.

"Augusta National is [the NCWO's] true target," Johnson said at the time. "It is therefore unfair to put the Masters' media sponsors in the position of having to deal with this pressure. It's not their fight."

Burk attempted to push CBS into dropping its coverage of the Masters, an attempt that the network never took seriously.

Sean McManus, the president of CBS Sports, told Burk that not televising the Masters "would be a disservice to fans of this major championship."

In October 2002, Burk announced that she planned to conduct a protest outside the gates of Augusta National during Masters week.

In November, Johnson broke a four-month stretch in which he'd remained silent, meeting individually with representatives from the *New York Times*, the Associated Press, the *Augusta Chronicle* and *Sports Illustrated* at Augusta National to spread his and the club's message. The news organizations were each given an hour to interview Johnson and agreed to embargo their interviews until 9:00 PM on November 11.

ESPN.com broke the embargo by running the AP's Q&A with Johnson in the afternoon, in which he said the club had no intention of admitting a female member by April, that it had no timetable for doing so, and that 99 percent of the membership agreed with him.

In a *Wall Street Journal* op-ed piece, Johnson wrote, "The notion that Augusta National is an enclave of sexist good old boys is ludicrous," and that the club would continue in its "resolve not to be told what to do by an individual who knows nothing about us."

With Masters week approaching, Burk submitted an application for a permit to demonstrate in Augusta in early March of 2002. It was for 200 protesters across the street from the main gate of the club on Masters Saturday.

On the surface, the demonstration was a disaster. It took place a half-mile down Washington Road from the club and it looked more like a series of depressing carnival acts than a serious demonstration.

There was an inflatable pig and an Elvis impersonator. There was a Ku Klux Klan Imperial Wizard named J.J. Harper and a flag-draped drag queen named Georgina Z. Bush.

"Augusta is all about Applebee's and boredom, so we certainly livened up the place," Burk told reporters. "The protest did not net the result that we wanted but beyond that, we accomplished our goal. We kept the issue in the media for a year. We wouldn't be talking about it now if not."

Influence

It's difficult to argue that Burk did not become one of the most influential figures in Augusta National history with her activism in 2002.

Though there is no hard evidence backing this up, it's very likely that Burk's work influenced several significant upgrades the club made for its Masters week experience in an effort to improve its image.

The Par-3 Contest, which annually includes players having their young kids caddie for them, is now televised live. A "Drive, Chip, and Putt Contest" was started for young boys and girls. And, in 2019, the Augusta National Women's Amateur was born. Both events take place in the two days before the Masters begins.

The most tangible evidence of Burk's influence on Augusta National came in 2012, when the club announced that Condoleeza Rice, a former Secretary of State, and Darla Moore, a South Carolina financier, were invited in as its first two female members.

"This is a joyous occasion," Augusta National chairman Billy Payne told the Associated Press the day the two women became members.

"Oh my God, we won," Burk told the AP.

Even Johnson, who had since retired as chairman in 2006 and died in 2017, said of the news in a statement to *The State* newspaper in Columbia, South Carolina, "This is wonderful news for Augusta National Golf Club and I could not be more pleased. Darla Moore is my good friend, and I know she and Condoleezza Rice will enjoy the Club as much as I have."

Payne, who took over for Johnson as chairman in 2006 (and was replaced by Fred Ridley in 2017), said consideration for new members was deliberate and private and that Rice and Moore were not treated differently from other new members. Still, though, he took the rare step of announcing two of the latest members to join because of the historical significance.

"These accomplished women share our passion for the game of golf and both are well known and respected by our membership," Payne said in a statement. "It will be a proud moment when we present Condoleezza and Darla their green jackets when the club opens this fall. This is a significant and positive time in our club's history and, on behalf of our membership, I wanted to take this opportunity to welcome them and all of our new members into the Augusta National family."

Significant figures in the game quickly began to weigh in.

Woods, who knew Rice through a connection at Stanford University, where he went to school, said in a statement, "I think the decision by the Augusta National membership is important to golf. The Club continues to demonstrate its commitment to impacting the game in positive ways. I would like to congratulate both new members, especially my friend Condi Rice."

Upon the news of Rice being admitted into Augusta, Woods also had a snide message for me, since I was the reporter who'd written that *New York Post* column calling him out as a hypocrite after that press conference at the 2002 British Open. Woods and his handlers were livid at the column, and Woods never forgot.

During a practice round for the PGA Tour's FedEx Cup Playoff event at Bethpage Black in 2012, Woods quietly made a beeline to me from the fairway as I followed his practice round and said sarcastically, "Well, you must be happy about Condi Rice getting into Augusta."

Ten years later, Woods had not forgotten that column I wrote and couldn't help himself from taking a dig at me.

Jack Nicklaus, who owns the record for most Masters victories with six and is an Augusta member, said, "Everyone at Augusta National shares a similar passion for the game of golf, and I know they will be great additions to the club."

Tim Finchem, the PGA Tour commissioner at the time, said, "At a time when women represent one of the fastest growing segments in both playing and following the game of golf, this sends a positive and inclusive message for our sport."

The Associated Press quoted sources who said that Rice and Moore first were considered as members in 2007, which would have been four years after the 2003 Masters, when Burk's protest took place, and one year after Payne took over as chairman.

"It came sooner than I expected," Burk told the AP. "I thought they were going to try to outlast me, and I really thought they would wait until the women's movement would get no credit. But if we had not done what we did, this would not have happened now."

Rice was the national security advisor under former president George W. Bush and became secretary of state in his second term. She was the first black woman to be a Stanford provost in 1993.

Since her admittance to Augusta, she has been very visible during Masters week wearing her green jacket. She's become good friends with the likes of Phil Mickelson, who plays golf with her on occasion and annually has lunch with her and some other members during Masters week on the veranda of the clubhouse.

"I have visited Augusta National on several occasions and look forward to playing golf, renewing friendships, and forming new ones through this very special opportunity," Rice said in a statement released by the club upon her admittance. "I have long admired the important role Augusta National has played in the traditions and history of golf. I also have an immense respect for the Masters Tournament and its commitment to grow the game of golf, particularly with youth, here in the United States and throughout the world."

Moore in the 1980s with Chemical Bank became the highest-paid woman in the banking industry. She was the first woman to be profiled on the cover of *Fortune* magazine, and in 1998 she made an initial $25 million contribution to her alma mater, the University of South Carolina, which renamed its business school after her. She later gave the school an additional $45 million in 2004.

"Augusta National has always captured my imagination, and is one of the most magically beautiful places anywhere in the world, as everyone gets to see during the Masters each April," Moore said in a statement upon her admittance. "I am fortunate to have many friends who are members at Augusta National, so to be asked to join them as a member represents a very happy and important occasion in my life. Above all, Augusta National and the Masters tournaments have always stood for excellence, and that is what is so important to me."

This all seemed a long way from Hootie Johnson's words to the Associated Press in 2002 when he defiantly said, "Our club has enjoyed a camaraderie and a closeness that's served us well for so long, that it makes it difficult for us to consider change. A woman may be a member of this club one day, but that is out in the future."

While proud of whatever difference she made, Burk, over the years, has not sounded completely satisfied with the change at Augusta National, actually remaining rather cynical.

In a 2013 article by Burk in the *Huffington Post*, she wrote: "Condoleezza Rice looks like she's having a great time—and more power to her. Someone emailed me to ask if I didn't think she maybe owes me a beer. Sure she does—me and a lot of others standing in that muddy field a decade ago. If we hadn't been there then, women wouldn't have the right to network with their big-business peers and play those manicured greens now."

This was a passage from what Burk wrote in another *Huffington Post* article ahead of the 2015 Masters: "The Green Dinos at Augusta National Golf Club will wine, dine, and brag about how their club is so exclusive the membership roster is secret. Well, mostly secret. If someone shows up at the tourney sporting a new green jacket, that means they've been allowed into the hoariest of old boys clubs.

"Augusta finally opened the gates a crack in 2012 and let two women squeeze through. It was hardly a breakthrough. The club famously snubbed Virginia Rometty, the new CEO of main tournament sponsor IBM, even though the male CEOs before her at Big Blue had been promptly welcomed into the fold. Last November, the boys relented and let Rometty in. In 25 years, will there still be only three token women?"

In a 2015 interview with *Sports Illustrated*, Burk said, "I definitely lit the fuse in changing Augusta National. They would be closed to women right now if we hadn't done what we did."

PART SEVEN

SUNDAY

Chapter 21

THE SHARK

G olf can be a cruel game. Augusta National sometimes can make it even crueler. Ask Greg Norman.

The pioneering Australian, who became known as the "Great White Shark" for his dominating prowess on the golf course and off it as an entrepreneur, was reduced to a minnow at Augusta National.

Twenty-three times Norman played in the Masters and 23 times he walked away disappointed, and sometimes devastated. No player in the Masters history has had more gut-wrenching close calls without reward than Norman. No player in the history of the game has been more associated with epic failure at a single major tournament than Norman at the Masters.

Norman was the bridesmaid to Jack Nicklaus' remarkable sixth career green jacket victory in 1986 at age 46. He was tied with Nicklaus after carding a birdie on the 17th hole. He hit his tee shot on the par-4 18th into the fairway, but pushed his approach shot into the gallery and bogeyed the hole, leaving Nicklaus to win by one stroke.

He stood helplessly on the 11th hole and watched Larry Mize, a likeable Augusta native, chip in from 45 yards for birdie and a playoff walk-off victory in 1987, Mize's only career major championship win.

None of Norman's close calls, though, were more painful than 1996, when he let a six-shot lead leak agonizingly away in the final round to lose to Nick Faldo.

Even if you were not rooting for Norman, that one was painful to watch for everyone who witnessed it, even Faldo, who copped his third green jacket at Norman's expense. On the way off the 18th green on the Sunday, Faldo, who'd shot 67 to Norman's staggering 78, consoled Norman as if his foe had just lost a family member.

Faldo, known for his aloof, stoic demeanor, had tears in his eyes as he and Norman walked off the 18th green, his arm around Norman. And those tears surely were as much for the man whose will he'd crushed as for his own accomplishment.

"I feel for him," Faldo said afterward. "What he's been through is horrible. It's hard to be plastered and repair that. He's had a real rough ride. I hope I'll be remembered for shooting a 67 on the last day and storming through. But obviously, it'll be remembered for what happened to Greg."

Norman, who was vying to become the first Australian to win a Masters (Adam Scott later would become the first, in 2013), owns the dubious distinction as the only player to lose all four major championships in a playoff.

As a closer, he was no Mariano Rivera. He won only one of the seven majors he led entering the final round. Nicklaus, by comparison, won 10 of the 12 majors he led after 54 holes.

"I played like shit," Norman said. "That's the best way to say it. I wouldn't like to see a player do what I did. Nobody would. I screwed up. I put all the blame on myself. People can write and say whatever they wish, but it wasn't nerves or impatience.

My rhythm went haywire. That happens in golf. But this mess-up came at the worst of times.

"I didn't choke, although critics will say I did. I just played rotten while Nick was playing great golf. I just screwed up. I never felt tight. Never felt tension in the body or the mind. No tension in my game."

As memorable as what happened on the golf course that day was the way Norman conducted himself afterward. He was classy, accountable, dignified, and even a touch defiant.

"I just didn't win today," Norman would say afterward. "I'm not a loser. I am a winner. I'm not a loser. I'm not a loser in life. I just lost a golf tournament. Maybe there is a reason for what I have inflicted on myself. Maybe something good will happen to me. All this is just a test."

Norman still had a five-shot lead through the fifth hole, but there was a sense that he wasn't right. Faldo birdied the sixth and eighth holes and those, combined with Norman bogeys at the ninth, 10th, and 11th, put them in a tie.

Norman's wedge approach shot spun back off the green on the ninth, leading to bogey. At the 10th, a poor chip led to another bogey. And at 11, Norman thought he'd made his birdie putt, but saw it slide by and he then missed the comebacker for par, taking another bogey.

"It was evident he was ruined through the middle of the round," Faldo said. "That's what really opened the doors up. I just had to play my game and keep the pressure on."

Norman insisted, "I never felt tight. The only thing I felt was I lost my rhythm. I lost my timing a little bit. I didn't feel any tension. I just played poorly."

Fittingly, it was at Amen Corner where it effectively ended for Norman, who hit his tee shot into the water at the par-3 12th and took double bogey, leaving him two shots behind Faldo. He never would recover.

"I felt it slipping away at No. 12," Norman said. "I knew it was gone at No. 16 (where he also hit his tee shot into the water). I let it get away. I'm very disappointed. Of all of them I let get away, this one I did let get away. Even if I had played halfway decent, it would have been a good tussle with Nick. I let it slip. I made a lot of mistakes. I just didn't get the job done."

No player had squandered a larger 54-hole lead in a major championship since 1910. Perhaps it was fitting that this Norman sunk ship came on the 84th anniversary of the sinking of the Titanic. Honest.

Mickelson, who finished third, said, "My heart goes out to him because he's an excellent player and a true champion and it just wasn't his day. I don't know what the deal was. He played excellent golf the first three rounds. It's hard for me to imagine that 78."

Nick Price, a close friend of Norman's, was finished with his round and in the clubhouse watching on a television and he finally had to look away, saying, "I can't even watch."

"If this were my last Masters, I'd be disappointed that I'd never won," Norman said. "It's the greatest championship in the world. God, I'd love to put on a green jacket, but it's not the end. I'm going to play here again, and I'm not going to fall off the end of the Earth.

"I'm very, very philosophical about things. That's one of my strong points, that I can approach life in that regard. Hey, of course I screwed this one up bad. It's definitely the most disappointing round of my career. But not everything's perfect your whole life. Maybe these hiccups that I've inflicted on myself are meant for another reason. I mean, that's how I think. I think there's something good waiting for me down the line."

As level-headed as Norman was, his fellow players were devastated for him, perhaps putting themselves in his shoes and shuddering at the mere thought of such anguish.

"This is tough for him; you have to feel terrible to lose a lead like that," Duffy Waldorf, who finished tied for fifth, said. "I felt he was uncatchable. I figured he could have shot even-par and still won. I don't think anybody else really thought they had a realistic chance to catch him."

Scott McCarron said, "It's kind of hard to feel sorry for Greg because of all that he's done, but you had to today because he had it in the bag. I guess those things happen at the Masters. But Greg's the best player in the world, and he's still the best. He's going to win this tournament someday."

Someday, of course, would never come for Norman at Augusta.

"I will awaken Monday morning, I trust, and will get down to Hilton Head to go on with PGA Tour work," Norman said. "My life is pretty good. It's not the end of my world, losing this Masters."

The Big Lead

A 1-under-par 71 in the third round on Saturday had Norman in the driver's seat, sitting comfortably with a six-shot lead at a tournament where no player had ever blown a six-shot lead in its 59 previous editions.

It was, however, the seventh time that Norman had entered the final round of a major with a lead, and he'd won only one of those, the 1986 British Open.

"I don't live in the past," Norman said on that Saturday. "I don't dwell on those things. I feel comfortable."

Norman's 54-hole total of 203 had him standing at 13 under par, with the Masters scoring record of 17 under (set by Jack Nicklaus in 1965 and tied by Ray Floyd in 1976) within reach.

"I'll try to come to the first tee feeling as comfortable and relaxed as I have the first three days," he said. "I'll treat it as if nobody is in the lead, pretend we all have the same score. I feel pretty good, but I've still got a lot of work to do. There's no sense getting excited now. I'm going to enjoy tomorrow no matter what happens. I'll try to enjoy it every step of the way.

"Irrespective of what happens, I'm going to enjoy every step I take. I've got a chance to win the Masters. I've been there before. There's no better feeling than having a chance to win a major championship."

Faldo, who was six shots back after Saturday, said, "I'm a long way back, but anything's possible. It's all gain and nothing to lose. Just go out and play."

Through three rounds, Norman had only one bogey on the back nine and 11 birdies. He'd birdied two par-5s on the back, No. 13 and No. 15, in all three rounds.

Asked on Saturday if anyone could catch Norman, Phil Mickelson said, "Well, I don't know. What do you think? I think that anything's possible, so I don't want to rule out the improbable."

Those turned out to be prophetic words from Mickelson.

————

A Letter

In the aftermath of Norman's Masters collapse, Scott Hoch sent a letter to Norman. The crux of the message: Been there. Done that.

"I felt terrible for him," Hoch told the Associated Press. "I was one person who could definitely commiserate with him."

Seven years earlier, Hoch was standing over a two-and-a-half-foot putt to win the Masters in a playoff with Nick Faldo. Hoch missed the putt and Faldo went on to win the first of his three green jackets on the next hole.

While Norman, perhaps because of all the major championship calamity he'd endured, was a sympathetic figure in the wake of that Masters loss, the media wasn't so sympathetic toward Hoch.

"They stabbed me pretty good," Hoch said.

When Hoch lost his close-call Masters, he joked to reporters that if he had a gun, he might have shot himself. A columnist followed that up by writing that it was a good thing he didn't because, with his aim, someone in the gallery could have been hurt.

"They [the media] weren't sympathetic toward me like they were toward Greg," Hoch recalled. "I thought they were kind of easy on [Norman]. He received what he should have, but they were pretty rough on me. All I did was miss a two-foot putt after playing awfully well the rest of the day. He played poorly all day."

Hoch won six times on the PGA Tour and won millions of dollars, but he never won a major championship, which makes that missed Masters opportunity one that he'll never forget.

"I don't know if you ever get over it," he said.

Norman, ever the optimist, tried.

When he returned to Augusta a year later, Norman revealed that he'd spent some time before that 1997 Masters with motivational speaker Tony Robbins, he of late-night infomercial fame.

Robbins visited Norman's house days before that Masters carrying an 800-page dossier on Norman.

"Tony's very motivational," Norman said at the time. "He doesn't want to get into your head and tell you how to play the game. He's never played the game. He doesn't know anything about the game. But he understands how to motivate people. What I got out of it was just reminding myself of who I am and how good I am, because you forget about all that. I was re-educating myself. That's all I was doing."

Part of the Robbins therapy was getting Norman to purge the bad times from his mind and focus on the good things he'd done—like the rounds in the low-to-mid 60s he'd shot at Augusta and not the 78 he threw down in the final round in '96.

"If you keep thinking about the worst round you've ever had in your life, you're going to keep playing that same crappy round," Norman said. "Flush it out. I don't want to keep thinking about it."

Norman later conceded that in the immediate aftermath of the loss, his collapse did adversely affect him.

"I was very angry with myself that day," Norman said of the final round. "Monday I was fine. Tuesday I was very angry with myself just for the emotion of everything. By the time I got back in the office and got home, it was gone. I am a very resilient guy. It's going to take a bigger bullet than that to stop me."

He recounted his annual spring vacation going deep-sea fishing in Mexico on his 87-foot yacht, Aussie Rules. He said the only round of golf he played was for fun, saying, "I drank 18 bottles of beer on 18 holes and had a great time."

Norman, who said he got more than 7,500 letters of encouragement from people, said the loss "changed my life."

"Each and every one of them had a meaning," Norman said. "It makes me feel better to be a father. My kids look up to me now. I am not as cynical now. I feel totally different about my whole approach to life and the world. I know I am a better person for it. I know I'm not a loser, as I said after the Masters. I know I have a lot of golf left in me. People have their perceptions.

They want to call you a choker or gagger. But in reality, they are not the ones there.

"The bad thing is that I didn't win," Norman went on. "The good thing is that it changed my life. I've never felt anything as powerful. It was a huge emotional lift, an overwhelming experience. I feel like I'm a different person now. A better person. Sometimes you get better things from not winning. This has definitely made me feel better. It was probably the tonic I need to carry on until I retire."

Chapter 22

SPIETH

Augusta National makes some players, and it breaks others. Jordan Spieth is one of those rare players who's experienced both extremes, and they came a year apart. Spieth won the Masters in 2015, and he should have won it in 2016, but he choked. That's right: he choked.

There's no shame in that. More accomplished players than Spieth, who's one of the great young players of the current generation, have thrown away major championships as their throats tightened in the cauldron of intense pressure and expectation.

One year after Spieth captured the 2015 Masters, he stood on the 10th tee in the final round with a five-shot lead.

And did not win.

———

Nine Holes Remaining

The tournament was over.

The final result of the 80th Masters was a foregone conclusion.

The only chore that seemingly remained for Spieth, who looked like he owned the tournament from his opening tee shot Thursday, was a trip to Butler Cabin, where he would slip the green jacket over his own shoulders as the defending champion.

Then all hell broke loose around Amen Corner.

Spieth, 22 at the time, was poised to win his second consecutive Masters and take over the No. 1 world ranking.

And then he did neither.

When the violent tornado had finally passed through Augusta National on an unforgettable Sunday afternoon, it had turned the tournament upside down and left Englishman Danny Willett, who, playing ahead of Spieth, quietly carded a final-round 67, as the winner at 5-under par and Spieth a stunning distant runner-up at 2-under.

Everything changed for everyone involved on No. 12—the centerpiece of Amen Corner and arguably the most famous par-3 in golf. In a shocking turn of events, Spieth authored one of the greatest collapses in not only Masters history but in major championship history when he took a quadruple bogey 7 on No. 12.

The carnage began with Spieth hitting his tee shot into Rae's Creek.

"It's a stock 9-iron for me," Spieth said. "I didn't take that extra deep breath and really focus on my line on 12. Instead, I went up and I just put a quick swing on it. It was a lack of discipline to hit it over the bunker coming off two bogeys, instead of recognizing I was still leading the Masters.

"Boy, you wonder about not only just the tee shot on 12, but why can't you just control the second shot, you know, and make 5 at the worst, and you're still tied for the lead?"

Incredibly, Spieth recalled making a similar mistake at No. 12 in 2014, when he took bogey and ended up finishing second.

"I remember getting over the ball thinking I'm going to go ahead and hit a little cut to the hole, and that's what I did in 2014 and it cost me the tournament then, too," he said. "That was the right club, just the wrong shot. I was more comfortable hitting a draw with my iron. I knew every time I played a fade this week, that shot kind of came out. At the time, you're going to throw all bad swings away and you're just going to focus on how confident you can step into that shot and that's what I did. But the swing just wasn't quite there to produce the right ball flight. So ultimately I should have just played a draw on that hole."

After the first ball in the creek, Spieth took a penalty drop in the shallow portion of the 13th fairway and chunked his next shot into the middle of the water—a shot you'd expect to see from a nervous 20 handicapper afraid to hit over a water hazard.

His fifth shot landed in the back bunker and, after he splashed out and made the putt, Spieth had scored a 7 on the hole—the highest score he'd ever posted in a major championship.

To put it in further perspective, Spieth had needed only eight strokes to play the par-3 12th hole during his first three rounds and seven shots on Sunday to complete it. As agonizing as it was for Spieth to experience, it was agony to watch—for everyone, whether they were witnessing it in person or from the safety of their couch on television.

"It just kind of stunk to watch it," said Smylie Kaufman, who was paired with Spieth in the final round.

"I can't imagine that was fun for everyone to experience—other than Danny's team and those who are fans of him," Spieth would say later.

"I think the whole golfing world feels for Jordan Spieth," Jack Nicklaus posted on his Twitter account. "He had a chance to do something truly special and something very few have done before—and be the youngest to accomplish that—and he just didn't pull through. My heart goes out to him for what happened, but I know that Jordan is a young man who will certainly learn from this experience and there will be some good that comes out of this for him. He's a wonderful talent and a wonderful young man."

Spieth carried a five-shot lead as he made the turn thanks to consecutive birdies on Nos. 6, 7, 8, and 9, and he looked in complete command. "It was a dream-come-true front nine," he said.

But he began to show signs of nerves with bogeys on No. 10 and No. 11. And then 12 happened.

"Just a lapse of concentration on 12 and it cost me," he said.

It cost him a chance at history, a chance to become only the fourth player ever to defend his Masters title.

Spieth, who finished second in his first Masters in 2014, and won it in 2015, entered the day having owned the lead in his previous seven rounds at Augusta, a Masters record. None of that mattered by about 7:15 PM, when Spieth staggered off the 18th green looking like he'd just gone 10 rounds with Mike Tyson in his prime—three shots behind Willett, the accidental-tourist winner.

"It's all rather surreal right now," Willett said.

Spieth was gutted afterward.

He had converted his previous five 54-hole leads into victories—two of those major championships.

"It was just a very tough 30 minutes for me that hopefully I never experience again," he said.

As he stood on the 12th tee, Spieth was 5-under par and had a one-shot lead over Willett. When he walked off the 12th green, he was 1-under par trailing Willett by three shots. He made a couple of game comeback birdies on Nos. 13 and 15, but never fully recovered.

"It all happened very, very quick," Willett said.

Jason Day said he was on the 15th hole when he looked at the scoreboard and saw the carnage. "I was absolutely shocked when I saw Jordan go from 5 to 1," Day said.

"Anything can happen at Augusta—especially at Amen Corner," said Lee Westwood, who tied for second with Spieth at 2-under. "It's a fine line between disaster and success at this place, and it happened to Jordan. Championship golf can throw in some shocks sometimes."

As if what he'd endured during the final 90 minutes of the tournament was not painful enough, taking part in the traditional green jacket ceremony at Butler Cabin and then on the 18th green must have felt like it took 90 days to Spieth.

"I can't think of anybody else who may have had a tougher ceremony to experience," Spieth said.

In a quiet moment during the green jacket ceremony, Willett, the son of a vicar in England, told Spieth that "maybe fate" had decided this was his time.

"I certainly wanted to control fate myself," Spieth said.

The Masters so often shows even the best in the game that they cannot control their own fate.

"Big picture, this one will hurt," Spieth said. "It will take a while."

Fortunately, for him, it would not take long, as he would exorcise any final-round major-championship demons he had with a win at the British Open in 2017.

———

In Position to Win

It sometimes is difficult to breathe when you're in rarefied air.

This was the challenge Spieth faced while trying to defend his Masters title in that final round. The way he performed in 2015—winning five times, including two major champion-ships—Spieth raised the bar so high you wondered whether he would need an oxygen mask to breathe.

His ascent to the top of the golf world gave him a glimpse into the world where Tiger Woods once resided. It is a world of unrealistic expectations that can sometimes suffocate those who are expected to succeed every time they show up. It is a world created by special athletes whose performances are so dominant they can become victims of their own success.

Woods lived in this world for a decade and a half and he thrived in it. Spieth was a visitor to that world and found it rather hot inside.

Spieth was attempting to become only the fourth player to defend his Masters title. He, too, was trying to win his fourth major championship at the age of 22. This is how Spieth's career Masters record would have looked if he were able to close that 2016 Masters out: runner-up, win, win. Had Spieth sealed the deal, he would have gone wire-to-wire to win the Masters for the second consecutive year. Preposterous stuff.

But Sunday would not come without its challenges. His late free-fall in the third round brought a few players back into contention for the final 18 holes. He had been cruising with a four-shot lead when he stepped to the 17th tee and pushed his drive into the right trees and took bogey. Then, on 18, he hit his tee shot even further right into trees and made a sloppy double bogey.

Suddenly, his four-shot lead was melted to one over Kaufman, two over the remarkable 58-year-old German grinder Bernhard Langer and Japan's Hideki Matsuyama, both of whom were 1-under. World No. 1 Jason Day, Dustin Johnson, and Willett, all deemed afterthoughts before Spieth's late hiccups, were just three shots back at even-par.

"I've got to throw this away, pretend [Sunday] is a new round and everyone is tied and understand that this is the position I wanted to be in after 54 holes and not think about the end to [Saturday's] round," Spieth said after his Saturday round. "It was a really tough finish to go from really holding a four-shot lead and being in a very similar position to last year to where all of the sudden now it's anyone's game. It's tough to swallow that.

"I'm in the lead after 54 holes. If you told me that at the beginning of the week, I'd be obviously very pleased."

The year before, Spieth took a commanding four-shot lead into the final round and cruised to victory. The vibe entering Sunday would be quite a bit different. "I certainly felt better last year on Saturday night than I do right now," Spieth said.

"He's been in control of this golf tournament from the first day," said Rory McIlroy, who was paired with Spieth in the third round. "I haven't got a green jacket. He has. So, there's added pressure that comes with that, too. So, we'll see what happens. He's sitting on top of the leaderboard...so it's his to lose."

So it was.

And it all came unglued on the 12th hole, a hole that Jack Nicklaus once called "the most dangerous par-3 in the game."

The 12th hole at Augusta has altered many lives in the past. Tom Weiskopf posted the highest score in Masters history at the hole when he took a 13 on it in 1980. The great Arnold Palmer hit into Rae's Creek in 1959 and it cost him a chance at a second consecutive victory.

The most notorious implosion on No. 12 came from Norman in 1996, when he took double bogey en route to losing a six-shot final-round lead to winner Nick Faldo.

So, Spieth was not alone.

As Spieth walked to his courtesy car in the players parking lot following the devastating loss, Faldo—of all people, the beneficiary of gifts from Norman and Hoch helping him win Masters green jackets—stopped him to offer words of encouragement and shake his hand.

"Greg was right from the word go on a downward trend, and Jordan was on an upward trend," Faldo told reporters that night.

Indeed, Norman already was well into his collapse by the time he and Faldo got to the 12th hole. For Spieth, the quadruple on 12 was so sudden.

Making what happened on the back nine, particularly No. 12, so shocking was that Spieth had closed out the front nine with four consecutive birdies to seemingly put the tournament to sleep.

Then came bogeys on Nos. 10 and 11, which could have been viewed as mere hiccups...until 12 happened.

"At 10 and 11, you can take bogeys there," Spieth said. "I was still 2-under for the tournament with a couple of par-5s left. My goal for the day was 4-under. So we were still right on pace. I just didn't take that extra deep breath."

The first shot in the water didn't cost Spieth. Like in the case with Phil Mickelson en route to blowing the 2006 U.S. Open at Winged Foot, where he famously hit his tee shot on the final hole off a hospitality tent, it was the second shot that doomed Spieth.

Like Mickelson's ill-advised 3-iron that he greedily tried (unsuccessfully) to bend around the trees and up toward the green, it was Spieth's chunked wedge after his drop that killed him. "I'm not really sure what happened on the next shot," Spieth said.

On his walk from the 12th green to the 13th tee, his lead turned into a deficit, Spieth said to his caddie, Michael Greller, "Buddy, it seems like we're collapsing."

Spieth was correct about that except for the tense of his sentence. He should have used the word *collapsed*, because by then it was over.

"This is going to hurt badly," Faldo said. "He was on the steps of doing something to join our little club, which would've been great. I would've welcomed him to our little club of those who have defended. The good news is he's 22. You regroup. He's way too talented. He's got a lot of majors he's going to have a shot to win."

———

Famous Masters Meltdowns

1996: Greg Norman lost a six-shot lead, the largest blown 54-hole lead in tournament history, as Nick Faldo shot a final-round 67 to win his third green jacket.

2011: Rory McIlroy began the final round with a four-shot lead and shot 80 to finish tied for 15th. McIlroy came unglued on the back nine, beginning with the 10th hole, where he yanked his tee shot so deep into the woods to the left of the fairway it was near the cabins.

1956: Ken Venturi failed to hold onto a four-shot lead in the final round, shooting 80, and lost to Jack Burke Jr.

1979: Ed Sneed began the final round with a five-shot lead and still led by three with three holes to play, but he bogeyed 16, 17, and 18 and Fuzzy Zoeller won in a playoff in his first Masters.

1986: Seve Ballesteros, rattled by Jack Nicklaus' famous back-nine charge, hit his approach shot to 15 in the water, opening the door for Nicklaus to win his 18th and final major.

1961: Arnold Palmer, needing only a par on the 18th hole to win back-to-back Masters, double-bogeyed the 72nd hole, allowing Gary Player to become the first international champion.

1989: Scott Hoch missed a short par putt on the 17th hole and then, on the first hole of a sudden-death playoff, he missed a two-foot putt that would have given him his first major championship win. Faldo took advantage and made a long birdie putt on the next hole to win his first green jacket.

1980: Curtis Strange had a three-shot lead with six holes to play in the final round and hit into the water on Nos. 13 and 15, finishing two shots behind winner Bernhard Langer.

2009: Kenny Perry had a two-shot lead with two holes to play and he left a putt short on the 72nd hole and lost in a playoff to Ángel Cabrera.

———

Aftermath

About a month after his Masters nightmare, Spieth related a funny story about the public reaction he'd gotten from people when they meet him.

"I've got ladies at the grocery stores putting their hand on me and going, 'Really praying for you. How are you doing?'" Spieth said. "I'm like, 'My dog didn't die. I'll be okay. I'll survive. It happens.'"

When Spieth returned to Augusta for the first time after the 2016 loss, in December 2016, he played with some friends and twice birdied the 12th hole, named Golden Bell.

"The first time back, I was very nervous when I got on the 12th tee," Spieth conceded. "I was playing with friends and I was vocally expressing that, 'Guys, we have some demons to get rid of here, I'd appreciate if y'all stood to the side of the tee box while I do my work here.'

"I hit an 8-iron over the bunker to about 15 feet and my putt fell in for 2. I probably gave like a big fist pump. I was walking around with my hands up, like, 'Demon's gone!' We played it the next morning and I hit a 9-iron this time to a left pin, and it landed about three feet beyond the hole and almost went in. So the last two times I played the hole, I made birdie."

Spieth has not won the Masters since his 2015 triumph, but the demons from 2016 are seemingly gone. Still a young man, he'll undoubtedly have many more chances to win another green jacket.

Chapter 23

RORY

Rory McIlroy has it all.
He's a multi-millionaire 10 times over.

He's happily married.

He has a strong family support system, with parents who've always been by his side and gone out of their way to enhance his chances to become a professional golfer.

He has multiple homes.

He has four career major championships.

He has it all.

Everything except a Masters green jacket.

Among McIlroy's four career major championships are the 2011 U.S. Open, the 2014 British Open, and the 2012 and 2014 PGA Championships. But no Masters, the only victory that separates him from becoming only the sixth player in the history of the game to complete a career Grand Slam by winning each of the four major championships. Only Gene Sarazen, Ben Hogan, Jack Nicklaus, Gary Player, and Tiger Woods have done it.

The lack of a Masters victory is probably the most confounding thing about the too-good-to-be-true twentysomething from

Northern Ireland, because McIlroy should have won at least one Masters—the 2011 iteration, to be precise—but probably a couple more as well.

The question, which still has years remaining before it can be answered based on McIlroy's youth and talent, is whether he becomes one of those bits of Masters history remembered for all the wrong things. A more modern-day Greg Norman, for example. Norman, of course, probably owns the record for most close calls at Augusta National without a trip to the Butler Cabin post-tournament for his own green jacket fitting.

McIlroy, at age 21 and precocious as ever, let the 2011 Masters slip through his hands. At that moment, it felt like a failure to meet great expectations from a golfing prodigy in one of the biggest collapses a major championship had ever seen.

McIlroy carried a four-shot lead into the final round after going 12-under-par for 54 holes but soared to a stunning, tear-filled 80 that left him 10 shots behind South African winner Charl Schwartzel.

"I'm very disappointed at the minute, and I'm sure I will be for the next few days," the classy, curly-haired McIlroy told reporters after the carnage was complete. "But I'll get over it."

Not since Norman squandered a six-stroke lead going into the final round of the 1996 Masters to finish five shots behind champion Nick Faldo had there been such a stunning final-day reversal at Augusta National.

McIlroy showed some early nerves, missing three putts of six feet and closer, but still clung to a one-shot advantage heading into the homeward half. That, however, is when things began to get ugly.

McIlroy hit a monstrously wild drive at the 10th on his way to a triple-bogey, 3-putted for bogey at 11 and 4-putted for double-bogey at the par-3 12th.

"I just hit a poor tee shot on 10 and I just sort of unraveled from there, just sort of lost it 10, 11, 12, and couldn't really get it back," McIlroy would say later. "It's one of those things. I've got to take the positives, and the positives were that I led this tournament for 63 holes."

The 10th hole was the most famous and most photographed of the day's slide. McIlroy pulled his tee shot into the woods to the left where a pinball-like ricochet off trees sent his ball between two of the Augusta National residential cabins that are dotted around the course and rarely seen during the championship—by fans or television cameras.

In the television shots and still photographs of McIlroy back near those cabins, miles off the 10th fairway, he looked like a boy lost in the woods, unable to process where he was or what was happening to him—even with his caddie, J.P. Fitzgerald, by his side doing everything he could to settle his player down.

After hooking his drive into the pines, McIlroy tried to hit a fairway metal on his next shot and it went wildly left once again. An attempted punch-out to the fairway on the next shot caught the limb of an overhanging tree.

When it was all over, McIlroy took a triple-bogey 7 that dropped him from first place to a tie for seventh, and it was all over. After not taking a single 3-putt in the event, McIlroy used seven putts on the next two holes to seal his fate. After hitting 9-iron onto the green on No. 12, he 4-putted.

"I can't really put my finger on it," he said. "I lost a lot of confidence in my putting around the turn. I didn't really get anything going and was sort of second-guessing lines and second-guessing my speed. On these greens you can't do that."

By the time he got to the par-5 13th hole, his round—and championship hopes—already long run off the rails, McIlroy had tears in his eyes after he hit a ball into Rae's Creek.

It was all such a shift from the McIlroy we'd been talking to during the week, the McIlroy who was laughing about the soccer and football games he and his best mates, Ricky McCormick and Mitchell Tweedie, were playing after the golf at the home they were renting near the golf course. It was an utterly carefree McIlroy, seemingly about to win the Masters at age 21.

And then he was en route to throwing away seven strokes in 12 holes. And he seemed so alone doing it.

With McIlroy having his boyhood friends with him that week, his parents, who usually traveled with him to big tournaments, stayed home and watched it on TV.

"Rosie and I didn't go because he was taking his mates that week," Gerry, recalled. "Now I sometimes say to myself, 'Maybe I should have been there.' But that's hindsight."

Tweedie recalled the agony of watching from outside the ropes.

"It was tough for us to watch," he said. "As it was going on, we kind of understood what was going on. He dealt with it very well. That's just him. I'd probably have my putter wrapped around someone's head."

Stephen Crooks, the Holywood head professional at the time, watched from home as McIlroy unraveled with a triple-bogey on the 10th hole, a 4-putt double on 12, and a drive into the creek on 13.

"On the 13th tee, I wanted to be there and give him a hug," Crooks said. "I just really felt sorry for him, because he knew at that stage it was over. Americans, who I know loved him to that point, but after what happened to him and the way he handled himself everyone just fell in love with him."

Paul Gray, the Holywood Golf Club general manager, called the way McIlroy handled himself at Augusta "very brave."

"Between walking off that 18th green and signing his score-card, I think he made the decision subconsciously that this was the starting point for getting over this and putting it behind him and moving on," Gray said. "It's not who he was."

McIlroy, at such a young age, showed his maturity by trying to put the painful experience in perspective afterward with this reasoning: "I'll have plenty more chances. I know that."

At that moment, it felt like McIlroy was trying to talk himself into that possibility as much as he was trying to talk everyone else around him into it. But he had finished in third place in three of the previous five majors and had looked to be heading for a Masters victory. So there certainly was reason to be opti-mistic—about that Masters and many more to come afterward.

Among the many lessons learned from that for McIlroy there was one that resonated most: when he took that four-shot lead into the final round, McIlroy changed his demeanor. And the move backfired.

"I came out and was trying to be this player that I'm not," McIlroy said. "I was trying to be ultra-focused, tunnel-visioned, which just isn't like me. I'm usually pretty chatty and sort of looking around and being quite relaxed about the whole thing. However you've played those first three days, try not to change anything. You just have to try to be the same person."

McIlroy called his worst career day on a golf course "very disappointing," but added, "Hopefully, it'll build a little bit of character in me, as well."

Runner-up Adam Scott of Australia called McIlroy "a hell of a player," adding, "He just needs to let it get out of his system and reset everything and get on with it."

Schwartzel, the winner that week, said, "Golf is a really funny game. One moment you're on top of it and the next it bites you. He's such a phenomenal player. He'll win one."

Will he?

McIlroy would tie for 40th in 2012, the year after the debacle. Then there was a tie for 25th in 2013. He finished tied for eighth in 2014, was solo fourth in 2015, then a tie for 10th, seventh, and fifth followed in 2016, '17, and '18 before a tie for 21st in 2019.

Of course, there's plenty of time for McIlroy to win a Masters and complete the career Grand Slam, but will there always be baggage for him when he drives down Magnolia Lane?

———

Early Years

McIlroy was a mere 2 years old when he first hit a golf shot some 40 yards with a plastic club that his dad Gerry had bought for him.

By the time he was four, he was chipping balls along the halls of his house, which was located across the street from the local golf club, Holywood, and into his mom, Rosie's, washing machine. Gerry had built a synthetic putting green that took up almost all of the small back yard.

Gerry McIlroy, a scratch golfer who'd been a member of Holywood since he was a boy, took on a second job as a bartender at night to raise enough money so he could send his boy to big international tournaments once it was determined Rory was, indeed, that good.

McIlroy used to hit balls for hours from the 17th tee, which is located right outside a clubhouse window. It was just outside that bank of clubhouse windows where McIlroy's remarkable journey to the top of the golf world began.

On a small practice tee next to the 17th tee, McIlroy first started hitting golf balls with Gerry by his side. Now, some 20-plus years later, if these windows could talk, they could have warned the rest of the golf world what McIlroy had in store for it. If those windows could talk...they saw a lot over the years.

"This is where is all started," Gerry McIlroy said, sitting at a clubhouse table sipping a cup of coffee a week before the 2011 British Open. "It seems like yesterday...."

Incredibly, two months after the Masters meltdown, McIlroy won the U.S. Open by eight shots at Congressional Country Club. After he had rebounded from that horrible Masters loss, that win, his first career major championship, would put a stamp on his resilience.

McCormick, the assistant pro at Holywood, said, "We all felt a bit sorry for him at the time on Sunday [of the Masters final round]. Looking back now, and certainly after the U.S. Open, it was a great learning curve for him and even better that it happened to him this early on in his career. He's learned a lot from it and learned a lot about himself as well."

McIlroy later would acknowledge what his close friend McCormick said.

"I learned so much about myself and what I needed to do the next time I got into that position," McIlroy said of that harrowing Masters loss. "If I had not had the whole unravelling, if I had just made a couple of bogeys coming down the stretch and lost by one, I would not have learned as much. Luckily, it did not take me long to get into a position like that again [at the U.S. Open two months later] when I was leading a major and I was able to get over the line quite comfortably. It was a huge learning curve for me and I needed it, and thankfully I have been able to move on to bigger and better things."

McIlroy took the U.S. Open trophy back to his hometown of Holywood, which sits in the shadow of Belfast just 10 minutes east. The day after McIlroy shocked the world with his record-shattering U.S. Open win, the local bakery in town, Skinners, made buns and cupcakes with a clear image in the icing of McIlroy holding the trophy.

"We did it for a day as a novelty and after the first day we said, 'Let's keep doing it,'" Wilson Skinner, the bakery owner, said. "We sold over 4,000 of them."

The irony of McIlroy growing up in Holywood, pronounced the same as Hollywood in California, is he is the furthest thing from the glitz-and-glam type.

To the locals in Holywood, McIlroy will always be that skinny, undersized kid with the freckles and the unruly thatch of brown hair doing otherworldly things with the golf ball since he was old enough to stand on his own two feet.

To a degree, McIlroy's early development as a golfer resulted from his mother, Rosie, working overnight shifts as a production line worker at the local 3M factory making tape. When Rosie returned home from work to sleep, that left Gerry, who started his bartending shift at 6:00 PM, to look after Rory in the mornings.

So he did what any golf-crazed dad would do: he took Rory with him to the golf club and let him watch while he hit balls.

"My earliest memory of Rory was looking out that window and seeing Gerry over at the practice tee on 17 and Rory sitting there while he was looking after him during the day," recalled Gray, the Holywood general manager who grew up playing at the club and worked his way up as the assistant pro and head professional. "As soon as Rory was able to get out of the buggy, he had plastic clubs and was knocking it around the club. It wasn't too long after, when he was three, that he had this little proper golf swing."

Gerry knew early on there was something special about his son's golf skills and focus, saying, "Rory was determined. You just know. Rory always wanted to just get better from when he was a young age."

When Rory reached 8 or 9 years old and needed to travel to competitions around the world, Gerry worked three jobs while his wife worked the overnight shift. They took their vacation time in the summer to bring Rory to tournaments in Hawaii, California, and Florida.

"If we hadn't worked so hard to get the money to send him to those golf tournaments, I could have been sitting back here today asking myself, 'Why didn't I do that?'" Gerry said. "We've been lucky it paid off for him."

Gabby Maguire, who has been running the restaurant and bar concession at Holywood Golf Club since 1998, recalled a Senior Cup match at Holywood, when the custom was to have the players and their opponents announced at a dinner the night before the event. Rory was 13, playing against the best adult players in the club.

"They called out this big guy from the club first and then they announced, 'Rory McIlroy,' and Rory walks out and the guy starts laughing," Maguire said. "[The match] was all over on the 13th. The guy obviously didn't know about Rory back then. I guarantee you that guy's not laughing anymore."

Maguire said he was first taken aback by the magnitude of Rory's fame when the club invited a group of military men from a nearby base to play in a competition. After playing, the servicemen were in the clubhouse for dinner, and McIlroy was playing that evening.

"The guys saw him out the window on the 17th tee box and they stopped eating their meals," Maguire said. "Rory drove the green [356 yards] from the tee box and these guys are watching this. Later, Rory came in and autographed golf balls for the guys, who've been through an awful lot in Afghanistan and Iraq. And they're like kids, melting like putty because they were in the company of Rory McIlroy.

"It was only then when I realized how big Rory is to other people—even though he's still just Rory to us."

Rory's uncle, Colm McIlroy, Gerry's younger brother, remembered taking Rory to a course in Belfast to play every Sunday in the winter. It was him, Gerry, a friend, and Rory.

"He was always miles behind us off the tee, obviously just a wee small fellow," Colm said. "Then one day, when he got to be 13, all of a sudden we're walking up to our drives and there were a couple bunched together and there was one 10 yards ahead. And we're going, 'God, that's Rory.'

"He got to his ball, looked back and said, 'Everything all right back there, guys?' He was only just over 5-foot then."

When Colm saw Rory a few days after his U.S. Open win in 2011, Rory was showing the championship trophy around the club.

"I shook his hand, gave him a hug and I said, 'Well done, Rory. I suppose I can't call you Wee Hacker anymore,'" Colm said. "He said, 'Not for a few weeks, anyway.'"

Despite the great success and wealth McIlroy has already achieved, from the accounts of those who know him best and have observed the way he conducts himself in the public spotlight, the young champion's humble nature might be his best trait.

Gray has heard McIlroy relate how when he was younger, he was just playing golf and not thinking much about the sacrifices his parents made for him.

"But when he looks back now, he realizes his life and his dad and mom's life are so different," Gray said. "I think he appreciates it a lot more now that he's older and gotten to where he's gotten to. He realized he couldn't have gotten there without them. The people around him have obviously had a massive effect on him."

Among those people are his best friends, who remain his closest confidants—McCormick, Tweedie, Paul Dorrian, and Harry Diamond, who's since taken over as McIlroy's caddie.

"Money doesn't matter to Rory," Gerry McIlroy said. "He doesn't change, and I'll tell you why: when he was growing up, we used to say to him, 'The only way to go through life is to be nice. It doesn't cost you any money to be nice.'"

The first thing you notice around Holywood Golf Club is all the young kids toting their carry bags. They all are respectful of the game and visitors, and they make you immediately envision Rory as one of them not long ago.

"They're all buzzing at the moment, excited by it all," Gray, the club general manager, said. "Rory has set a bar, an achievable vision for them, I suppose. Rory has taken the bar from here and put it to the top of the world. They're looking up to the best that any human being can possibly be at golf. They have him as a role model from their own golf club."

Gray described the feeling in Holywood about McIlroy's success as "a mix between just so much pride and disbelief."

"Looking back, everyone expected Rory could do it, but you've got to pinch yourself sometimes to think that the U.S. Open champion came from your little club in Northern Ireland," he said.

Gray paused and looked out those clubhouse windows, as if again envisioning Rory at age two hitting balls on that practice tee with his dad, way back at the beginning of this magical story.

"Looking back on what happened in the 2011 Masters, it doesn't seem as bad when you have four majors on your mantelpiece," McIlroy said. "If I was to look back as a 60-year-old at my career and had not won a green jacket I would be very disappointed. It is the only one left and it is a course I feel I can do well at. I feel I could win multiple times, but getting that first one is the most important thing. Winning all four majors means you are a complete player. I can achieve something special."

———

Tiger Influence

McIlroy was drawn to the game by watching Tiger Woods' record-shattering 12-stroke Masters victory in 1997, and he vowed he would one day do the same.

Among the records the younger McIlroy amassed are becoming the youngest winner of the West of Ireland Championship and the youngest selected for the Walker Cup. At age 16, he set the course record on the demanding Dunluce links at Royal Portrush, where the 2019 British Open was played, in 61. The scorecard is immortalized behind glass doors on the first floor of the clubhouse.

As a nine-year-old, he sent a letter to Woods announcing, "I'm coming to get you. This is the beginning."

McIlroy had just won the 1998 Doral-Publix Junior Golf Classic in Florida for the 10–11 age group, and Woods was the No. 1 ranked player in the world.

"He was someone I put up on a pedestal," McIlroy said of Woods. "Now I obviously have a very different relationship with him. I know him quite well. But I think if you ask a lot of golfers [of] my generation, he was the benchmark. He was the inspiration for us to go out and try to be the best that we could be."

After McIlroy won the world amateur championship and then won his first professional title, in Dubai in 2009, Woods splashed this praise on him: "He's got a lot of talent. We all know he has a lot of talent and it's just a matter of time before he starts winning a bunch of tournaments."

That's exactly what McIlroy has done. By 2019 season's end, he'd won 17 times on the PGA Tour, including his four majors. McIlroy, who pocketed the $15 million prize that came with winning the FedEx Cup Playoffs in the late summer of 2019, has won pretty much everything except a Masters.

And he's insisted that he won't obsess about that or worry about his career being defined by what he hasn't won. McIlroy always has been comfortable in his own skin like that.

"I think there's a difference between a personal desire and a need, and I think I've separated those two," he said. "I would have said a couple of years ago, 'I need to win a Masters. I need a green jacket.' But now it's, 'I want to. I want to win it.' And I'd love to win it. But if I don't, I'm okay. And I think that is the difference.

"I've become comfortable with the fact I've tried four times and I've failed," McIlroy said in advance of the 2019 Masters. "But Abraham Lincoln lost the first 13 elections he was ever in [and] he wound up being the president of the United States. So, I still got a bit of time."

McIlroy's facts on the number of elections Lincoln lost before becoming president of the United States were a little off—it wasn't that many. But his point was made.

"It's definitely taken me time to come to terms with the things I've needed to deal with inside my own head, and I think sometimes I'm too much a fan of the game because I know exactly who has won the Grand Slam and I know exactly the people I would be putting myself alongside," McIlroy said. "So that's maybe a part of [the pressure]. If I didn't know the history of the game and I wasn't such a fan, it would work in my favor. But that's not me.

"[A Grand Slam] would be a massive achievement. It would be huge. But again, I can't think of it that way. I just have to go out and play the golf course the way I know that I can play and repeat that for four days. And as I've said, hopefully that's good enough to have the lowest score that week.

"I feel like I'm good enough to join those people [Sarazen, Hogan, Player, Nicklaus, and Woods], and that it would just be a very proud moment in my life and something that I could look back on, and I would love to sit at the Champions Dinner when I'm 92.

"Believe me, I am motivated to make the most of what I have and to put my name among some of the greats of our game. I'm going to try my ass off there, and I'm probably not going to win. I've had 10 years of learning at Augusta, some tough times. And if one day I'm able to get that green jacket at the end of 72 holes, all of those experiences will have played a part in helping me do that. So, have I a desire to do it? Yes. Do I have a need to do it? No."

Chapter 24

TIGER, 2019

The grill room inside the Augusta National clubhouse was standing-room only on the Sunday afternoon of the 2019 Masters.

Everyone's attention was fixated on two television sets in separate corners of the room, focused on every move Tiger Woods was making on the back nine in what was unfolding into one of the most memorable conclusions in tournament history.

Underneath one of the TVs sat Tiger's family. His mother, Tida, nervously sipped tea. His two children, son Charlie and daughter Sam, noshed on candy, oblivious to the historic goings on around them. Woods' girlfriend, Erica Herman, was so fidgety that Justin Thomas' mother, Jani, sat down next to her and clutched Herman's right hand as if she was about to give birth.

History hung heavily in the air inside that grill room and around the Augusta National grounds, and it certainly wasn't lost on Woods' loved ones, who were more keenly aware than anyone about the struggle he'd endured to get to this place.

This place: a 15th career major championship, a fifth career green jacket, the end of an 11-year drought without a major and 14 years removed from his last Masters victory.

Something many—including Woods himself—believed would never happen again happened on Sunday at Augusta.

And this one erased a pesky asterisk from Woods' remarkable career resume in that it was the first major championship he's won when trailing entering the final round. Woods already had been lauded as the greatest closer of all time—the Mariano Rivera of his sport. But he'd never chased someone down in a major championship final round.

Until that Sunday.

"Just unreal," Woods would say after overtaking 54-hole leader Francesco Molinari with a frenetic final-round 70 that got him to 13-under par for the week, one better than Brooks Koepka, Dustin Johnson, and Xander Schauffele, and two better than Molinari, who closed with a 74, Jason Day, Webb Simpson, and Tony Finau.

"I had serious doubts after what transpired a couple years ago," Woods said of the four back surgeries he'd endured. "I could barely walk. To have the opportunity to come back like this...it is probably one of the biggest wins I've ever had for sure because of it."

Adding to the sweet taste of this victory was the fact that it was Molinari whom Woods was paired with in the final round at the British Open in July of 2018 at Carnoustie. Woods took the lead on the back nine only to watch the steely and steady diminutive Italian overtake him and hoist the Claret Jug.

This time, the final round turned in favor of Woods and against Molinari on the 12th hole, the par-3 centerpiece of the fabled Amen Corner. For the first 11 holes, there were no signs that Molinari was going to give anything back. He'd been too steady, just like he was at Carnoustie nine months earlier.

And then Molinari pushed his 8-iron tee shot into Rae's Creek on the 12th, took double bogey, and everything changed.

Woods was now tied for the lead at 11-under par and the smell of victory was intoxicating to him—as evidenced by his birdies on 13, 15, and 16, where he came within inches of a hole-in-one, to seize control of the tournament.

"There were so many different scenarios that could have transpired on that back nine," Woods said. "There were so many guys that had a chance to win. The leaderboard was absolutely packed and everyone was playing well. You couldn't have had more drama than we all had out there, and now I know why I'm balding. This stuff is hard."

The birdie on No. 13 gave Woods his first final-round Masters lead since 2005, the last time he'd been fitted for a green jacket.

"It didn't feel unfamiliar because I had the lead at the Open Championship, so that was just two majors ago," Woods said. "I just kept saying, 'I've been here, it wasn't that long ago. Just go ahead and just keep playing your game, keep plodding along and keep doing all the little things correctly.'"

The birdie on 16 gave Woods a two-shot lead and Augusta National, which is a place of decorum—where fans are called "patrons" and no running is permitted on the grounds—was off the rails.

"I birdied 13, I birdied 15 with two good shots in there, and almost whooped it at 16," Woods said. "That gave me the cushion, and I kept telling myself on 17, that tee shot, I said, 'I've been in this position before. I had a two-shot lead with [Chris] DiMarco and went bogey, bogey [in 2005]. Let's go ahead and pipe this ball right down the middle.' I hit a little flat squeezer out there and I did, I just smoked it.

"Then on 18, I said, 'Hey, it's not over yet. Arnold [Palmer] once lost the tournament and lost the hole with a double. So let's keep the hammer down. Brooksy could still make birdie up 18 and I could make bogey and next thing you know we're in a playoff, so let's get this ball in play.' I did that, and I saw [Koepka] tap out for par [on 18], and that gave me the cushion knowing that I could make bogey."

Which he did, which was enough to win comfortably.

"I just felt so prepared coming into this event," Woods said. "This year, my finishes don't really reflect it, but I was starting to shape the golf ball the way that I know I can, which I needed for this week. Prep for the Masters started six months ago, so just trying to make sure I get ready to peak for this one week, and I did, and everything came together, which is great.

"I kept doing all the little things correctly. Missed the ball in the correct spots time and time and time again, and if I was out of position, so be it, take my bogey and move on. I had no doubles this week. Just kept, as I said, just kept plodding along."

By the time he plodded off the 18th green, suddenly, one of the world's most famous and snooty golf clubs felt a lot more like Yankee Stadium with fans chanting, "Tiger, Tiger, Tiger," as Woods fell into the arms first of his caddie, Joe LaCava; then his son, Charlie, whom he squeezed so tightly you worried for the child's health; then his daughter, Sam, with whom he had a long, emotional embrace; then Herman.

"It hasn't sunk in at all," Woods said afterward. "It's going to take a little bit of time."

Woods has said for the past couple of years that his biggest motivation was to win a major in front of his children now that they're old enough to understand the magnitude of the moments. He said all they'd associated golf with was the pain it had been causing their dad.

That Sunday was the first time Charlie and Sam had been to Augusta National, the place where Woods formally introduced himself to the world with his record-shattering victory in 1997.

"I hope they are proud of me," Woods said. "I hope they are proud of their dad. I've been very blessed to have two great kids, and just to have them here to see this and witness this...they have never been to Augusta National. This is a pretty unique event. This is very special. So it all worked out and here they are."

When Woods first started winning majors early in his career, his father, Earl, was a staple waiting for him at the 18th green for a congratulatory hug. By the late '90s, though, Earl's health began to deteriorate before he died in 2006. Earl was there in 1997 for his son's first Masters win for a tearful hug as Woods walked off of the 18th.

"My dad's no longer here, but my mom's here, 22 years later, and I happen to win the tournament," Woods said. "And then to have both Sam and Charlie here, they were there at the British Open last year when I had the lead on that back nine and I made a few mistakes, cost myself a chance to win The Open title.

"I wasn't going to let that happen to them twice," Woods said with a smile. "So, for them to see what it's like to have their dad win a major championship, I hope that's something they will never forget. I think the kids are starting to understand how much this game means to me, and some of the things I've done in the game. Prior to [the] comeback, they only knew that golf caused me a lot of pain. If I tried to swing a club I would be on the ground and I struggled for years, and that's basically all they remember. We're creating new memories for them, and it's just very special."

Woods said having his kids there to see him win "means the world to me."

"Their love and their support, I just can't say enough how much that meant to me throughout my struggles when I really just had a hard time moving around," he said. "Just their infectiousness of happiness [while] I was going through a tough time physically...there were a lot of times when I really couldn't move, and so that in itself is difficult. But just to have them there, and then now to have them see their Pops win, just like my Pops saw me win here, it's pretty special.

"This whole tournament has meant so much to me over the years. Coming here in '95 for the first time and being able to play as an amateur, winning in '97 and then come full circle, 22 years later, to be able to do it again, and just the way it all transpired and to have my family is something I'll never, ever forget."

Peers' Reaction

As euphoric as the patrons around the grounds were, the reaction of Woods' fellow competitors was astounding.

"I'm just ecstatic for golf and I'm ecstatic for Tiger," Zach Johnson, the 2007 Masters winner, said. "We just witnessed history. It's raw, it's fresh, we're 10 minutes after the fact, so hear me out: I don't know what a better comeback in sports is. I'm sure there are probably ones you can argue. But in my lifetime, I don't think I've seen a comeback like this."

Woods' peers, all of them years younger than him and all of them inspired to become pros because of him, gathered at the clubhouse after Woods had put the finishing touches on his fifth career Masters win and first since 2005, first major championship win since 2008.

Rickie Fowler was there, along with Justin Thomas, Bubba Watson, Brooks Koepka, Xander Schauffele, and Johnson, to name a few. Even two-time Masters winner Bernhard Langer was there to witness it and congratulate Woods.

"I saw light at the end of the tunnel," Fowler said of Woods breaking through to win another major after the long, agonizing wait that included the multiple back surgeries, an addiction to pain-killers that landed him in rehab after a DUI arrest, not to mention his embarrassing infidelity scandal that very publicly ended his marriage. "I saw this as something that potentially could happen. I also knew the 15th major was going to be the hardest. Seeing how healthy he was and how much fun he was having playing the game a couple falls ago when we were at home, he had plenty to go win.

"I don't doubt that this is going to be his most special one...yet. To get his 15th after a long wait, after a lot of years away from competitive golf to be in position where he wasn't sure if he'd be able to play again...it's cool stuff."

Thomas, who like Fowler, plays a lot of golf with Woods in the Jupiter, Florida, area where they all live, also said he expected Woods to rise again in majors.

"I've played enough with him and know that he was playing well enough and I thought the final round was going to be big in how he handled it," Thomas said. "He's been there a lot, been there more than anybody, but it had been a while since he'd been there here, had a chance to win here. Whether he admits it or not, I'm sure this one is one of the most important or biggest [wins]."

Even Molinari, whom Woods vanquished on that final round back nine, sounded genuinely happy for the winner.

"It's great to see Tiger doing well, but the way he was playing last year I think we all knew it was coming sooner or later," Molinari said. "So maybe next time it will be better for me, but it was nice to be out with him. He played well, he hit the right shots at the right time and deserved to win."

Tony Finau, who was also in the final group with Woods, said the day before the final round that Woods' 1997 Masters win was the reason he took up golf. As he spoke, Finau held his young son in his arms and was asked what he'll tell him about the experience when he's old enough to understand.

"I'll tell him I was there in the final group when Tiger won his 15th major," Finau said. "At that point, I'll hopefully have a few under my own belt. This is something that I've dreamed of for a long time. I'm going to relish in the moment and enjoy being in contention at a Masters. As a kid, I always wanted to compete against him and have the opportunity of playing in the final group with him in a major championship.

"You can't say enough about Tiger and what he's done for the game. It's great for him to be involved in the game and now he's got his 15th major. He's going to be a force to be reckoned with these next few years, I'm sure."

Finau, speaking with the breathless enthusiasm of a kid who'd just gotten off his first thrill ride at an amusement park, called it "fun being a part of the action" as a part of the Woods final-round vortex.

"You can't beat the experience," he said. "It's something you can't pay for. When you're someone like me in my shoes still trying to come up, still trying to win majors, still trying to contend, you can't beat playing with the best player in the world, the best that's ever done it and just see if you can get the job done is cool. I wanted to get the job done, but Tiger is great for the game and again, unbelievable that he's winning his 15th major today.

"It was a lot of fun to be in that type of atmosphere. It's what I practice for, what I play for, what I train for. My time is coming. I know it is. I've just got to keep riding the storm."

Even in defeat as he searched for his first career major championship, Schauffele called that final round "an awesome experience."

"What I witnessed, I know it's what everyone is going to talk about for a long time," he said. "It was really cool coming down the stretch, all the historic holes, Amen Corner, 15, 16, Tiger making the roars. I was trying to push myself, but I feel like I got a very full, fully filled Masters experience here in my second year.

"With what we just witnessed with Tiger coming off 18, it was a throwback, seeing him in red in the mock turtleneck. It's what I saw as a kid, and it was just really cool to know him a little bit now and congratulate him coming off 18."

Brooks Koepka, one of the three runners-up to finish one shot behind Woods, said he was "happy for Tiger, after everything that's gone on, and it's cool to see."

"This is definitely probably one of the greatest comebacks I think anybody's ever seen," Koepka said. "That was probably the coolest back nine in a major championship I've ever been a part of. I don't know how it looked on TV, but it was amazing to be a part of. It was quite fun. I watch the leaderboard all the time to see where guys are at and what they are doing, and to see Tiger, what he did down the stretch was impressive. We already knew he was back, but I think he put the exclamation point on it.

"I think we all knew [another major] was going to come. I said it [in 2018] at the British, I thought he was ready, raring to go to win a major again and it only took him, what, two more tries? It's impressive, it's fun to watch and it's, as a fan, just of golf and of Tiger, it's very special. To be able to come back out here and have the Tiger of old back, as a fan, I love it. I'm glad he's back.

"It's probably one of the coolest things to be a part of it, even though I finished second place [and am] a little bummed out. But I wouldn't want it any other way. You want to play against the best to ever play. You want to go toe-to-toe with them. I enjoy the battle, I enjoy everything that goes on with it. It's what I watched as a kid. It's what I watched growing up.

"It was an incredible experience. He got the better of me this time. I'm sure he's ecstatic about it, but hopefully there will be a few more."

Eight months earlier, at the PGA Championship at Bellerive in St. Louis, Koepka staved off a furious Woods rally in the final round to win. It was there Koepka got his first true taste of Tigermania.

"The atmosphere around Tiger is mind-blowing, and to be inside the ropes and just kind of see it as another player is pretty cool and unique," Koepka said. "I heard it at the PGA. You hear it here [at Augusta]. You know any time he does something good, the fans are going to get excited and they are going to be loud, and that's the following that he's created. It's cool to see if you take a step back while you're playing. I mean, you watch him walk down after he won on 18 there, I mean, it was just a monsoon of people. It's incredible."

———

Turning Point

Amen Corner, one of the most storied and sacred grounds in golf, isn't famous for no reason. So it should come as no surprise that the par-3 12th hole, the centerpiece of Amen Corner, had a lot to say about the final outcome of the 2019 Masters.

Everything changed on the 12th hole Sunday. For Woods. For Molinari. For Koepka. And for Finau. The latter three hit their tee shots into Rae's Creek. Woods did not.

Four players in the last two groupings found the water off the tee at the 12th, including Molinari, who was two shots ahead of Woods at the time. Finau, also in contention and playing along with Woods and Molinari, also found the water and so did Koepka, who was in the group ahead of Woods.

All of them took damaging double bogeys on the hole, while Woods managed a par and never looked back from there on his way to victory.

Woods walked to the 13th tee tied with Molinari at 11-under, while Koepka went from 11-under to 9-under and Finau went from 10-under to 8-under.

Woods promptly parred the par-5 13th to take the lead, the first time he had a final-round lead in the Masters since 2005, and he never let go of it.

"That mistake Francesco made there let a lot of guys back into the tournament, myself included," Woods said. "There were so many different scenarios that could have transpired on that back nine. There were so many guys that had a chance to win. The leaderboard was absolutely packed and everyone was playing well."

Molinari lamented a poorly-executed 8-iron for his missed shot at the 12.

"I think we picked the right shot and just didn't hit it hard enough," he said. "It was a tough with the wind gusting. I managed to scramble well on the front nine. I just had a couple of mental lapses on the back nine that were costly. I think it wasn't my day today. That ball on 12, if it's one yard farther left it probably goes in the bunker.

"Obviously, I did a couple of things that I wish I had done differently. But I'll learn from my mistakes."

Molinari had bogeyed No. 11 in the first round and then went 49 holes without a blemish on his card until he got to the 12th on Sunday.

"It was probably 9-iron yardage, but I didn't want the wind to gust and get the ball too much," he said. "I just didn't hit it hard enough. Sometimes it's your day. Sometimes it isn't."

Finau conceded that the 12th hole, which with some swirling winds played as the most difficult hole on the course with a cumulative scoring average of 3.38, was the turning point.

"For me 12 was the turning point, that was the tournament," Finau said. "It's a hard shot. Not my best swing and it ended up costing me. Francesco had just hit it in the water, and I knew I just had to hit it on land. It was the perfect club for me. I barely hit it chunky and it kind of rolled on me. The line was okay, and I thought it had a chance to fly on the green and unfortunately it didn't.

"I knew from then on I had to play pretty much perfect golf. I still could have made something happen down the stretch. But 12 was kind of a big swing."

Koepka blamed a gust of wind for his water ball on 12, saying, "Once it gets above those trees, it's just a guessing game."

Woods?

"All I was concentrating on was I had 147 over the first tongue in the bunker there, and so my number, I was hitting it 150 and just be committed to hitting it 150," he said. "I saw Brooksy ended up short. Poults [Ian Poulter] ended up short, as well. So when I was up there on the tee box and it was about my turn to go, I could feel that wind puff up a little bit.

"Brooksy is stronger than I am and he flights it better than I do, so I'm sure he hit 9-iron and didn't make it. So I knew my 9-iron couldn't cover the flag, so I had to play left, and I said, 'Just be committed, hit it over that tongue in that bunker. Let's get out of here and let's go handle the par-5s.' And I did."

Woods, by far the most experienced of the players in contention, credited his experience for helping him make No. 12 the turning point in the round.

"It helps being around here and playing this golf course so many different times," he said.

Molinari's caddie Pello Iguaran perhaps captured the consequences of No. 12 and what it meant for Woods best when he said, "You cannot open the door to those kinds of great players. So you see what happens."

———

Moving Day

There's an unmistakable energy that engulfs a golf tournament—particularly a major championship—when Woods is merely in the field. The crowds are exponentially larger. The buzz on the grounds is palpable.

That energy when Woods is in contention to win a major is another story entirely. There are few things in sports like it. Think Super Bowls and heavyweight championship fights.

This is the high-voltage electricity that would grip Augusta National for Sunday's final round with Woods playing in the final group, two shots out of the lead held by Molinari.

The man Woods needed to run down and catch was the unflappable, steely-nerved Italian whom he failed to overtake the previous July at Carnoustie, where Molinari won the British Open despite Woods having taken the lead on the back nine in the final round.

Molinari and Woods were paired together and Molinari stared Woods down, didn't show as much as a quiver of intimidation as he, not Woods, hoisted the Claret Jug.

Molinari, who shot 66 in the third round and was 13-under par, again played with Woods in the final round, joined by Finau, who like Woods was 11-under par.

Koepka, winner of two of the previous three majors, was 10-under. Simpson and Ian Poulter were 9-under.

When it was pointed out to Woods on Saturday that he had a chance and that this was the closest he'd been to winning a green jacket in years, he said, "That was the plan and here I am."

"It's been a while since I've been in contention here," Woods said. "But then again, the last two majors count for something. I've been in the mix with a chance to win major championships [the British Open and PGA Championship] in the last two years. So that helps."

As it turned out, it would.

"If he brings the game he had today, we're going to see what kind of Tiger effect there is on this generation," David Duval said on the Golf Channel after that Saturday round. "Look at his eyes: they look like they did 10, 12 years ago. There's an intensity and also an ease with what he's doing."

Unlikely Comeback

Not long before that magical week in Georgia, Woods was not sure he'd ever be anywhere close to at his best again. What he would accomplish that Masters week felt unfathomable, unrealistic, impossible.

Two years earlier, Woods thought his career was over after the third back surgery didn't relieve his pain. But spinal fusion surgery on April 19, 2017, gave him a new lease on life, and golf.

"I had serious doubts after what transpired a couple of years ago," Woods said. "I could barely walk. I couldn't sit. Couldn't lay down. I really couldn't do much of anything. To have the opportunity to come back like this, it's probably one of the biggest wins I've ever had for sure because of it."

On the eve of that Masters, during the Golf Writers Association of America's annual awards dinner, Woods was the recipient of the GWAA's Ben Hogan Award, given to the player who "has overcome a physical handicap or serious injury to remain active in golf."

"Golf was not in my near future or even distant future," Woods told the audience that Wednesday night before the opening round of the 83rd Masters. "I knew I was going to be part of the game, but playing the game, I couldn't even do that with my son Charlie. I couldn't putt in the backyard. But playing the game again? I was done at that particular time."

Woods' back issues were so dire that he nearly wasn't even able to make it to the Masters Champions Dinner in 2017, even though he was unable to play in the tournament. He revealed that he had to take a pain-relieving "nerve blocker" injection just to be at Augusta for the dinner.

"I got there and didn't want to miss it," Woods said. "It was tough and uncomfortable."

It was at that dinner where Woods quietly confided to some people that he didn't think he was ever going to play again.

"I know he whispered to another Masters champion two Masters dinners ago [in 2017], 'I'm done. I won't play golf again,' and here we are, 18 months later," said Nick Faldo, a two-time Masters champion and current golf broadcaster who was at that dinner.

Woods recalled that the day after that 2017 Champions Dinner he flew to England to see a back specialist, who recommended that he undergo a spinal fusion. Woods decided to go through with the procedure, and it saved his career—and his life as a normal functioning human being.

"It was not a fun time and a tough couple of years there," Woods said. "But I was able to start to walk again, I was able to participate in life, I was able to be around my kids again and go to their games, go to their practices, take them to school again. These are all things I couldn't do for a very long time."

Woods wasn't able to make a full swing with a driver until September 2017 at the Presidents Cup in New Jersey, where he served as a non-playing vice captain. And even then, he joked that his first few drives traveled only 90 yards.

At the '19 Masters, Woods led the field in greens hit in regulation (83 percent) largely because he drove the ball so beautifully.

"It's the best I've felt with a driver in years," Woods said. "I was able to hit the golf ball both ways this week, and some of the shots I hit down 13, turn it around the corner, a couple of drives down 2, some of the bombs I hit down 3; and then to hit little squeezers out there down 7; you saw it today on 15 and 17 and even on 18, just little trap squeezers out there, as well.

"I was able to hit both ends of the spectrum, low cuts and high draws. That's not easy to do, so I just really felt that I had that much control in my long game and it paid off."

After he won, Twitter blew up with high-profile celebrity congratulations to Woods.

From former president Barack Obama: "Congratulations, Tiger! To come back and win the Masters after all the highs and lows is a testament to excellence, grit, and determination."

From current president Donald Trump: "Watching final hole of @TheMasters. @TigerWoods is looking GREAT!"

Another from Trump: "Love people who are great under pressure. What a fantastic life comeback for a really great guy!"

From Patriots quarterback Tom Brady, who's won six Super Bowls: "Running the numbers on how long it'll take me to get to 15..."

From Golden State Warriors star Stephen Curry: "Greatest comeback story in sports."

From tennis star Serena Williams: "I am literally in tears watching @TigerWoods this is Greatness like no other....I am so inspired thank you buddy."

Woods finished 13-under 275 for the week and became, at age 43, the oldest Masters champion since Nicklaus won his sixth green jacket at 46 in 1986. Woods' fifth Masters title moved him past Arnold Palmer and put him one behind Nicklaus for the most green jackets in history. Woods made his debut in 1995 and was the low amateur. He went on to win in 1997, 2001, 2002, 2005, and then 2019.

Woods, who had gone 28 majors over 11 years without winning before that 2019 Masters, set or tied 27 records when he won the 1997 Masters by 12 shots, including being the youngest winner at 21 years, three months, which still stands. Now he owns the record for length of time between Masters victories at 14 years. Nicklaus has the record for the length between the first victory and his last one, at 23 years. Woods went 22 years between his first and fifth wins.

"A big 'well done' from me to Tiger," Nicklaus tweeted. "I am so happy for him and for the game of golf. This is just fantastic!!!"

Fred Ridley, the chairman of Augusta National Golf Club and the Masters Tournament, called the final round "an epic Sunday and a great day for golf," adding, "It's one of the most amazing days in our history."

"Tiger, welcome back," Masters media chairman Craig Heatley, his voice cracking, said in his New Zealand accent as he introduced Woods in the post-round press conference. "Or should I say, more appropriately, welcome home."

———

18 in Play?

Golf is a numbers game. You try to shoot a number. You try to beat a number. The golf course has 18 holes and you try to conquer each of them.

After Woods' 2019 Masters victory, the newest, most relevant number for him again became 18—as in his pursuit of Nicklaus' record of 18 career major championship victories was back in play.

There was that time, back in the late '90s and early 2000s, when Woods was mowing down major championships, checking off boxes and ruthlessly moving on to the next thing. After his 2008 U.S. Open victory, the 11 years that followed without a major championship victory for Woods felt like an eternity for him and it felt like the end for the rest of us wondering whether he'd win another one. He was stuck on 14 majors and it seemed like that was going to be where the number stood forever—second to Nicklaus' 18.

And then the 2019 Masters happened.

It seemed like it hadn't been 10 minutes after Woods' final putt disappeared into the cup on No. 18 at Augusta and he hugged his family and friends greenside when everyone was ready to re-start the Woods–Nicklaus countdown.

"This keeps 18 in play," Fowler said, standing outside the clubhouse with Masters patrons still chanting Woods' name.

"Eighteen is, I think, a lot closer than people think," Koepka said. "I would say that's probably what all fans...what we're thinking—that he's definitely back and 18's not far."

Woods, after his first Masters win since 2005 and first major championship since 2008, was asked if he thought Nicklaus "should be worried" about Woods catching him.

"I don't know if he's worried or not," Woods said. "I'm sure he's home in West Palm just chilling and watching."

Can Woods win more majors?

Of course, he can.

Will he?

The chances improved greatly after Masters 2019.

If you don't think he'll be one of the favorites to win more Masters for the foreseeable future, you didn't pay enough attention to what transpired in April 2019, and specifically in that final round.

Nicklaus, in an interview on the Golf Channel the night of Woods' victory, said, "I don't ever pull against anybody. Nobody wants their record to be broken. But I certainly wouldn't want Tiger to be hurt and not to be able to do it. Of course, he is now pretty healthy and playing well. I wish him well. I always wish the guys well and I want them to play their best and don't want anybody to play poorly."

Nicklaus said as he watched Woods play the final round, he thought, "This is a man who is possessed. He is possessed to win the golf tournament. He absolutely under total control and he was going to get it done. There wasn't any question after my mind after seeing Molinari hit the ball in the water at 12 and Tiger put it on the green. I said, 'The tournament is over. It doesn't make any difference what anybody else is going to do. Somebody else is going to make mistakes, but Tiger is not going to make any.' And he didn't.

"You watch how smart he played and how he used his head at 12 and he put the ball in the middle of the green," Nicklaus went on. "How he put the ball to the left of the pin at 13. How he put the ball in the middle of the green at 14 and 15. How he put the ball to the right of the hole at 16 to use the slope. Right on the middle of the green at 17.

"What a nice, smart pitch shot on 18. He hit the pitch shot so it wouldn't roll through the green. He hit the pitch shot into the slope so it would come back. Every shot I saw him play was a smart shot. When you've got a guy who plays smart shots like that, plays them well and knows what he's doing and plays them with confidence, he should be your winner.

"I think he understands who he is, understands how to play the game, understands how to play smart, and how to play where you are not going to put yourself in a position to play bad. Tiger has been a terrible driver the past few years. He drove the ball magnificent [in the final round]."

Nicklaus added, "Everybody has been asking me about Tiger, 'Can Tiger win again? Will he win another major?' I thought for a long time that he was going to win again."

Asked if that win refocused his sights on getting to 18 majors, Woods said, "I really haven't thought about that yet. I'm sure that I'll probably think of it going down the road, but right now it's a little soon. I'm just enjoying 15."

Woods' caddie, Joe LaCava, also was not about to get ahead of himself.

"Before this, I never thought about 18 for him; I just thought about 15," LaCava said. "Now that he has 15, we'll think about 16. I always think the sky's the limit for the guy, but I don't think of 18 as a caddie. It's been a long time for him, a lot of question marks, injuries. Yeah, 10 years from now looking back, No. 15 probably was the hardest one for him to win."

Woods' biggest takeaway from the win was this: "I can win majors now," he said.

When he won the Tour Championship in September of 2018 at East Lake to end a five-year winless drought, Woods said that showed him he could win again. It all sounded so difficult to believe for a player who'd won 79 times, including 14 majors, at that time. But confidence is a fragile being, and even the greatest in the world needs a shot of it every once in a while for reinforcement.

"The win at East Lake was a big confidence booster for me because I had come close last year a couple times and I didn't quite do it," Woods said. "East Lake was a big step for me, confirming that I could still win out here and against the best players. My last three major championships have been pretty good, so that in itself gives me a lot of confidence going down the road."

Woods' Masters triumph left you to wonder whether his fellow players, the same players who gushed about his win at Augusta, unwittingly fell into a trap.

In the years that Woods struggled to find his game that won him that fifth green jacket, the younger generation of golfers who grew up watching him dominate and intimidate pined to have the chance to compete against him while he was playing like the major-championship-winning Tiger of old.

That magical week at Augusta, particularly in the final round, they got their wish. That begged the question: Should these players be careful what they wished for?

Woods, en route to winning that 15th career major and fifth Masters to end an 11-year drought without a major and 14 years since his last Masters victory, left those of that very younger generation in his wake on his way to the Butler Cabin to collect his fifth green jacket.

Is this an omen of things to come for Woods—and his current crop of competitors—now that he's broken through and proven to himself that he can resume winning majors again?

Back in his days of dominance, Woods broke the spirit of some of his nearest competitors while he was collecting his first 14 major championships.

Ernie Els, a perpetual major championship bridesmaid to Woods, was left baffled, frustrated, and at his wits' end. David Duval, who for a short period wrested the No. 1 world ranking from Woods, didn't last very long before his desire to compete for majors burned out. Vijay Singh took his lumps from Woods. How many more wins would Phil Mickelson have had it not been for his prime coinciding with that of Woods?

"The first golf tournament I ever watched was the '97 Masters," Finau said. "Just watching Tiger dominate the way that he did was very inspiring for me for some reason as a kid, and I took up the game the summer of '97, I think in huge part because of Tiger. Tiger taught us how to compete.

"We're the aftermath, if you will, of the 'Tiger Effect.' The way he dominated and watching him growing up, it was like he was scared of nobody. So, I think a lot of us try to be like him and try to be that way to where nothing on the golf course can scare us and our skills can showcase. He's playing against a different generation now. He's playing against guys that he kind of bred.

"We were watching him as teenagers through high school and watching him dominate, and I think all of us relish now having a chance to compete against him."

In the end on that final-round Sunday, it didn't work out so well for Finau. He hit his approach shot into Rae's Creek on the par-3 12th hole, as did Molinari, the leader at the time, gifting Woods a tie for that lead with double bogeys.

One hole later, a Woods birdie on 13, and he was in the lead he would never relinquish. Three holes after that, Woods birdied No. 16 to take a two-shot lead and the final two holes were a formality.

For those who followed Woods "back in the day," this was a familiar scene. Once he got the lead the tournament was over.

Did Woods' presence—the Tiger Effect—have any influence over how those players in contention around him failed to perform at their peak when the heat of pressure began to rise?

There's no tangible way to measure these things. But Finau did concede that a Tiger Effect remains in existence.

"I stay in my lane and do my thing no matter who I'm playing with, but there's always a Tiger Effect, no matter who you are," Finau said. "I'm not going to act like it's not there, because I know that it is."

For some of the younger players, like Schauffele, the experience around Woods is still a novelty. As such, he sounded a lot more thrilled at Woods breaking through to win his 15th major than he sounded devastated that he wasn't able to win his first.

"It's hard to really feel bad about how I played...because I just witnessed history," Schauffele said. "It's what I watched as a kid. It was like a dream, honestly."

Yes, but if Woods turns this Masters victory into another one of his historical runs through majors, that dream will turn into a nightmare for the likes of Schauffele, Finau, Fowler, Bryson DeChambeau, and the other young players who are seeking their first major championship and if they keep getting denied by their idol the way he denied the likes of Els, Duval, Singh, and Mickelson for all those years.

It, too, could affect those who've already broken through to win majors but crave more.

"I'm sure he feels like he has a great chance," Justin Thomas, a one-time major winner, said of Woods' chase of Nicklaus' record of 18 majors. "More importantly, I hope I can do something to stop it."

Chapter 25

THE CADDIE

T he very essence of who Joe LaCava is can be captured in the 15 frenetic seconds of Tiger Woods' celebration that immediately followed his fifth career Masters victory in April 2019.

Look at the TV clip: there's no immediate sign of LaCava in the frame while Woods wildly releases 11 years of frustration without a major championship victory with a series of emotional fist pumps and arms and putter thrust toward the sky.

When LaCava finally enters the frame, with Woods seeking him out for an embrace, Woods jubilantly screams to his caddie, "We did it!"

"No," LaCava responded to Woods. "You did it."

This is who LaCava is to his core. He's a background guy, not a "me" guy. Woods' former caddie, Steve Williams, who authored some of the most awkwardly misjudged high fives in sports history, always celebrated Woods' victories as if he was the one who had been making the shots. There always was an air of self-importance about Williams.

LaCava is about everything but self-importance

"I didn't put in all the hard work, I didn't have all the surgeries, I wasn't down in Florida grinding," LaCava said after

Woods' Masters win. "So, for me, it's easy. I just show up, try to do a halfway decent job and he has to do all the tough work."

That's not entirely true. It was LaCava who texted Woods days before they were to meet at Augusta to practice before the tournament began. He implored Woods to get to the course early Sunday to walk the holes with only a wedge and a putter to work on his short game, because that's what LaCava felt needed some last-minute work.

Woods later would credit LaCava for his prescience, citing how much his short game helped him win a fifth green jacket.

It was also LaCava calming down and pumping up Woods with some powerful words on the first tee of the final round. "Intense but loose," LaCava told him. "Don't carry the weight of the world on your shoulders."

Then it was LaCava giving Woods a stern talking-to after a second consecutive bogey on the fifth hole, a message that helped turn Woods' round around.

"The talk that Joey and I had off of 5—I just listened," Woods recalled. "Then I went into the restroom and proceeded to say the same things over and over to myself, and then came out and I felt a lot better."

LaCava is so much more than a "keep-up-and-shut-up" caddie toting Woods' bag around the golf course. He's an integral, trusted part of Woods' success and he's become a close friend, too, since they hooked up in 2011.

LaCava is a 55-year-old lifer in golf whose fierce loyalties are unbreakable, whether it's his rooting interest in the Giants and Rangers or his work with Woods.

LaCava, who wore a New York Giants running back Saquon Barkley T-shirt under his white caddie overalls during the final round at Augusta National last month, could have left Woods to work for another player at any time during the two years Woods was effectively sidelined with back surgeries. During one stretch when Woods' back limited him most, LaCava went 466 days without working.

Woods encouraged him to work for another player.

"He was suggesting to me—at least giving me the option—to go work for someone else," LaCava said. "He knows that I like to work and want to work, he knows how competitive I am and how much I do enjoy caddying. He also said, 'If you latch onto somebody full-time and you guys are hitting it off and doing very well together, I've got no problem if you go off riding into the sunset with that guy, and I hope it works out for you.'"

LaCava never considered it, choosing to ride it out until Woods would become healthy enough to compete again—despite how dire it looked at times.

LaCava, who's been with Woods for 10 wins, called Woods' loyalty to him "the same as I've been to him, if not more."

"He looked after me financially when he was out," LaCava said. "He'd send me some nice texts to check on me and my family when he was not playing for a long time. He also expressed, 'If you don't move on [to another player], terrific, I want to have you and I hope you stick around. I want you as my caddie when I do come back.' That meant a lot to me when I was sitting out."

The wait for LaCava has been well worth it. Woods' win at Augusta was a second career major championship for LaCava, who was on Fred Couples' bag when he won the Masters in 1992.

Perhaps the most emotional moment for LaCava and Woods came while they were in the scorer's room minutes after the 2019 win at Augusta.

"We just kind of looked at each other and soaked it all in," LaCava recalled. "We just took a deep breath. Nothing was really said. We got to share the moment and smile at each other. It was such an achievement, a proud moment more than anything.

Nothing needed to be said because we could read each other's minds."

LaCava said Woods later sent him a text message that read, "We did it, appreciate you hanging in there with me, I love you like a brother."

The byproducts of the Woods victory have been plentiful, including countless text messages from the likes of Chris Mara from the Giants, former Giants tight end Mark Bavaro, and former New York Rangers Brad Richards and Martin St. Louis, with whom LaCava is close.

"These are guys that I was watching on TV and respect the heck out of and now they're reaching out to me because they love golf," LaCava said.

LaCava has been a staple at Augusta National for some 30 years. The Connecticut native and lifer caddie has been with Woods for the bulk of Woods' attempted comeback, and he'd endured much of the heartache with Woods.

That 2019 Masters win, Woods' first major championship victory since 2008 and first Masters win since 2005, was a momentous occasion for both player and caddie.

"I'm just happy for him winning, because this one might have bought me a couple more months," LaCava said with his signature self-deprecation.

LaCava has become like family to Woods, often staying with him on his yacht (named Privacy) during tournament weeks and hanging out with him at his home in South Florida. LaCava is probably as paramount in importance to Woods' comeback as anyone.

The scene on No. 18 at Augusta with the crowd going bananas and Woods' mother, two children, and girlfriend waiting for him on the back of the green?

"It was a special moment," LaCava said. "He was typical Tiger. He said, 'We did it,' and I said, 'No, you did it. You played great.' Very special. I knew his kids were out here, so I thought that was even more special."

There was that moment before tournament week when LaCava quietly urged Woods to tweak his preparation routine, and that advice might have been a catalyst to the victory.

"[The previous week] I texted him and said, 'How about we get up there on Sunday afternoon with nobody around and chip and putt on one of the nines?'" LaCava recalled. "At that time, I thought that was the part of his game that needed the most work. I could tell once he took that to heart, he was like, 'I've got to work on my short game a little more and I've got to get after it.'"

LaCava, not the outward emotional type, described Woods as "pretty emotional and pretty jacked up" after the win.

"He thinks in the back of his mind that a lot of people doubted him," LaCava said. "I don't look at it that way. He's not trying to prove people wrong. He's just happy that he won."

As LaCava spoke in the aftermath of the Woods victory, he was leaning on the back of Woods' courtesy car, in which he'd just put the 18th pin and flag.

"I've got to get off the property before I get arrested," he joked.

He talked about his own feelings, about the reward for him sticking it out for so long with Woods when it looked so grim.

"I was sitting around thinking, 'This sucks sitting at home,'" LaCava said. "But it was all worth it."

The 2019 Masters was LaCava's first major while working with Woods. The only other major championship he'd won before in his career was that '92 Masters with Couples.

"I didn't want to be a caddie for only one guy that won a major," LaCava said. "I don't know if I dreamt about it, but I pictured it. I don't think I would have stuck around for as long as I did if I didn't think he wasn't capable of pulling something like this off. I mean, he is Tigers Woods after all, right?"

LaCava, as regular a guy as you'll find in the game, player or caddie, has played a big part in humanizing Woods, who had spent so much of his career building a reputation as untouchable, cold and aloof, and above it all.

"He's high-fiving people, talking to people, signing some autographs," LaCava said. "I think he's enjoying playing golf and being around people. He's much more fan-friendly, great with the kids. Everyone out there is pulling for him. He's enjoying it more."

A month after Woods' Masters victory, he was invited to the White House by president Donald Trump to be given a Presidential Medal of Freedom. LaCava and his wife, Megan, were invited by Woods to be a part of his small gathering of those closest to him.

"I wasn't surprised [to be invited], but certainly appreciative of the fact that my name was on the list and the list was somewhat small, and to include my wife as well was great," LaCava said. "He makes my whole family feel a part of the team, so that's a great thing for me. I feel fortunate to have the job that I have. I love working for the guy. I'm not going anywhere."

EPILOGUE

The day after the Masters has been played, once the green jacket has been awarded, there's a one-day tournament on Augusta National that isn't televised and that few people know about.

On the Saturday of the third round, 28 members from the media are selected—via a lottery system—to play Augusta National on the Monday after the tournament has been decided.

The experience is not unlike what it must feel like for a non-professional athlete to take batting practice at Yankee Stadium or play a couple sets of tennis on Centre Court at Wimbledon.

The pins are in the same places they were for the final round. Everything is the same as the final round except for the empty grandstands, and the media play from the members tees, not the championship tournament tees.

If you're lucky enough to be selected, you are given a small blue ticket stub with a number on it that looks like one of those coat check tickets you're given at a restaurant, and you are not permitted to enter your name back into the lottery for the following seven years.

It took me five years of covering the Masters before I was selected. It was 1998, the year Mark O'Meara won the green jacket with a 20-foot birdie putt on 18 sealing it, and it was an experience that was as euphoric as it was harrowing.

Here's how it went:

It was 7:15 in the morning Monday, and I felt like the luckiest person on the face of the earth at that very moment, because I was standing on the first tee at Augusta National with a driver in my hands.

I was the everyday, accidental-tourist hacker whom the powers that be in green jackets normally don't allow to roam their course. But my ping-pong ball came up in the annual Masters media lottery.

I came to Augusta National committing a cardinal sin: I came without my swing, which sometime in the previous two weeks had gone from somewhat dependable to shank city.

Battling the onset of the dreaded shanks before a dream round like this is worse than having a couple nasty cold sores pop up around your mouth the morning of your wedding.

But I played the course anyway, because it felt like a once-in-a-lifetime dream come true, the ultimate round of golf.

At that time, the driving range was not open to the Monday interlopers, so there was no time to practice before the most important round of my life, no chance to try to work my way out of the shanks. Club officials have since modified the day-after experience, allowing the players to be "members for a day," driving down Magnolia Lane, using the Champions Locker Room and the practice facility.

So at that time, without as much as a practice swing on that early Augusta morning with the sun rising and the dew evaporating, I striped my first drive over the corner of the right fairway bunker. I'd never felt so euphoric. It was as if I was skydiving for the first time. My playing partner said to me, "Is this really happening? Are we really here?"

The entire experience is surreal, something I wish every person with an enthusiasm for the game could be a part of just once.

Walking up that first fairway, my tracks straight up the hill were the first of the day, like a skier carving the first turns into fresh powder. I had chills. For years I'd watched the greatest golfers in the world walk this very route.

Now I was inside the ropes.

I was Tiger Woods without the entourage, without the zillion-dollar endorsement deals, and without talent.

Then it all went awry. My euphoria morphed into horror when I realized I simply could not get an iron airborne.

After my perfect drive on No. 1 that left me with 128 yards to the green in perfect condition, I warned my caddie, "You're going to see some unorthodox things today," referring to advice I once got from a local New York pro to hit balls with my heels together to get rid of the shanks. So, as ridiculous as it looks, that's the way I played.

I proceeded to click my heels together like Dorothy from *The Wizard of Oz* and cold topped an 8-iron underneath the trees to the right of the green and was so afraid of hitting another iron, I used my putter to punch out from the trees—something I guarantee no pro did during that Masters week.

I somehow managed a 49 on the front nine, and then, shortly after the turn, the round—and my fragile psyche—would unravel.

My anticipated foray into Amen Corner was a wildly disappointing ride, despite how awestruck I was by the magnitude of it all.

My waltz through Amen Corner, which went double bogey, triple bogey, triple bogey on Nos. 11, 12, and 13, was the most pathetic performance on that hallowed ground since Greg Norman sputtered around this legendary corner two years prior en route to famously leaking away his six-stroke lead to hand the green jacket away to Nick Faldo.

I hit a fat 8-iron approach shot into the water on 11, though after a drop I hit a crisp sand wedge to eight feet and holed the putt to save double bogey.

The most humiliating moment came on No. 12, the famous par-3 at Amen Corner.

There was a backup at the 12th, the favorite photo-op place for players, and when my turn finally came to hit, I could feel those people on the tee looking at me and thinking, "What is this imbecile doing with his heels together?" Those were my thoughts in mid-backswing. I shanked a six-iron so far right it landed in the 13th fairway. I wanted to slink into the woods and disappear.

I'd been holding the round together with duct tape and Band-Aids, but now the dam had cracked. I somehow got a pitching wedge shot into the back bunker. I took one step to the left and my caddie said, "No, we've got to go this way," and he wheeled me to the right. Every golfer wants to walk over the famous Hogan Bridge. But I'd hit it so far right, I had to walk over the Byron Nelson Bridge to get to the green. I never set foot on the Hogan Bridge.

Angered at the triple on 12, which included three putts from 10 feet, I roped a drawing drive up the right side with the beautiful contours of the 13th fairway and I felt better quickly. It was, albeit, merely a temporary moment of euphoria.

"Let's get a birdie on this hole," Mac Williams, my caddie with 23 years at Augusta National at the time, said to me. "Let's birdie this hole."

Easy for him to say.

With that, I promptly shanked a 5-iron right and then hit another 5-iron into Rae's Creek, winding up with a triple-bogey 8.

By the time I left Amen Corner, I was afraid of every club in my bag, as if each one were an enemy plotting to ruin my life.

I was a pitiful mass of humanity by No. 15, where I found yet more water. From the middle of the fairway after a good drive, trying to get the ball to the green on 15 with water in the front and back looks as difficult as trying to land a 767 onto the George Washington Bridge. It felt that tight.

How rattled was I at that point?

I looked at the "Through 14:" scoreboard along the 15th fairway and realized if my name was up there, it would read: "Through 14: Mark Cannizzaro +28."

It was a horrific performance at this golf cathedral, where the fairways and greens are perfect and without a weed in sight, and some of the bunkers with their white sand look like ocean waves rolling toward you.

I went from the euphoric feeling of being in heaven to the angst of hell in 18 holes, yet I'd never been so happy shooting a 113 after following my front-nine 49 with an unthinkable 64 on the back.

I was embarrassed by my performance, disgusted at not being able to produce my "A" game for what should have been the round of my life. But I also was grateful for having had the opportunity to have been there to do it in the first place.

A most fitting twist to my day: after putting out for yet another disappointing double bogey on 18 to finish my round, I dropped a ball to the spot where O'Meara drained his 20-footer to win the Masters the day before and nailed it dead center. It was the longest putt I hit all day.

I walked away desperate for another shot at Augusta National, because I felt I had a score or two to settle.

Two years later, I would get my chance to even the score.

After the 2000 Masters, I actually snuck my way onto Augusta National. I cannot tell you how, because I must protect my sources. Anyway, that's irrelevant. The point is, I was getting the chance to redeem myself with a round that began on the 10th tee.

That fateful April day in '98, stricken with a virus-like case of the shanks, I went around Augusta National with tears in my eyes because I had been reduced to a mass of frightened humanity.

When I left that day, I'd desperately hoped to play Augusta again. Someday. It was inhuman, after all, to subject a passionate golfer to a one-off chance while he's got the shanks. That's like bringing a starving guy with his jaw wired shut to a one-time-only all-you-can-eat lobster buffet.

Without as much as a practice swing, I crushed a drawing drive off the 10th tee that rolled to the bottom of the fairway hill at precisely 8:45 AM the morning after the 2000 Masters that Vijay Singh had just won.

I took a double on 10 despite the good drive and Amen Corner awaited. The iconic three-hole stretch I'd played in 8-over par two years prior. There were demons to be exorcised.

What would transpire for the next 40 minutes or so I can only theorize was by the grace of God. I was heroic through Amen Corner, where Singh nearly threw away the green jacket the day before.

I smashed a drive almost to the drop area on 11, punched a 7-iron to the front of the green and 3-putted from about 70 feet for bogey. Singh was in the water on his second shot the day before. I was on the green.

On 12, a place where I'd shanked a 6-iron so far right two years ago that I never got a chance to walk over the fabled Hogan Bridge, I stiffed a 6-iron over the Rae's Creek, over the bunker and onto the green.

After savoring the walk over the Hogan Bridge and entering the utter serenity of the 12th green, I fixed the ball mark from my shot (never have I taken such pleasure in fixing a ball mark in my life) and 2-putted for par.

On 13, I nuked another huge, drawing drive and had 220 to the pin. From there, I flushed a 5-wood over Rae's Creek and just off the green to the left and ended up parring the hole.

I'd settled the score; 1-over around Amen Corner—a seven-shot improvement from the last time I'd been there. This was one of the thrills of my life.

What I would do the rest of the round mattered little. I'd conquered Augusta's daunting Amen Corner.

I ended up shooting 97 (shaving some 16 shots off the previous effort). I finished the memorable day with only three pars and had 38 putts. But my performance on Amen Corner left me with immeasurable satisfaction. I left the grounds quietly and with a smile painted to my face as if it had been me, not Singh, who'd won the green jacket.

SOURCES

Newspapers and Periodicals

Associated Press

Augusta Chronicle

Huffington Post

Los Angeles Times

New York Post

New York Times

Pittsburgh Post-Gazette

Sports Illustrated

Wall Street Journal

Television

Golf Channel

Websites

Golf Channel.com

NJ.com

PGATour.com

ACKNOWLEDGMENTS

Special thanks to: Phil Mickelson, who was kind enough to write the foreword for this book and for being so generous with his valuable time being interviewed for it.

New York Post (particularly Greg Gallo, my first sports editor, and Chris Shaw, my current sports editor) for assigning me to golf, which has sent me to the past 25 Masters and more than 100 major championships in my 26 years at the newspaper.

Paul Azinger, who provides colorful and insightful analysis on anything and everything golf related...and on plenty of other topics, as well.

Scott Michaux and David "Ghost" Westin, both of whom worked tirelessly at the *Augusta Chronicle* for years delivering the most comprehensive coverage any annual big sporting event has ever gotten.

Charles Howell III, who is one of the most enjoyable and insightful interviews in golf.

Ernie Els, who is one of the most honest interviews in golf.

Mark Cumins, the owner of TBonz Steakhouse, the unofficial Masters 19th hole.

Tiger Woods, who's as responsible for me (and countless golf-writing colleagues) covering as much golf as I have since his dramatic arrival in 1997 and subsequent dominance since.

Oliver Katcher, who should own a patent on the Masters fan experience.

Also helpful through various interviews:

Brian Bush	John Daly
Scott Brown	Zach Johnson
Andy North	David Love III
Jim Nantz	Rickie Fowler
Joe LaCava	Nick Watney
Jim "Bones" Mackay	Brandt Snedeker
Keegan Bradley	Paul Casey
Jim Furyk	Peter Jacobson
Jack Nicklaus	Fuzzy Zoeller
Gary Player	Geoff Ogilvy
Tony Finau	Nathan Grube
Gary Woodland	Jay Danzi
Brendan Steele	Mark O'Meara
Jordan Spieth	Jimmy Roberts
Jason Day	Curtis Strange
Ian Poulter	Nick Faldo
Adam Scott	Patrick Reed

Bernhard Langer
Charl Schwartzel
David Duval
Justin Thomas
Xander Schauffele
Francesco Molinari
Brooks Koepka
Rory McIroy
Gerry McIlroy
Gabby Maguire
Colm McIlroy
Paul Gray
Danny Willett
Justin Rose
Sergio García
Angela Akins

Paul McGinley
Lee Westwood
Duffy Waldorf
Scott McCarron
Joe Damiano
Billy Payne
Greg Norman
Fred Couples
Colin Montgomerie
Steve Stricker
Costantino Rocca
Nick Price
Ben Crenshaw
Jimmy Walker
Webb Simpson
Morgan Hoffmann